WOMEN AND WORK

WOMEN AND WORLD DEVELOPMENT SERIES

This series has been developed by the UN-NGO Group on Women and Development and makes available the most recent information, debate and action being taken on world development issues, and the impact on women. Each volume is fully illustrated and attractively presented. Each outlines its particular subject, as well as including an introduction to resources and guidance on how to use the books in workshops and seminars. The aim of each title is to bring women's concerns more directly and effectively into the development process, and to achieve an improvement in women's status in our rapidly changing world.

The Group was established in 1980 to organize the production and distribution of joint UN-NGO development education materials. It was the first time that United Nations agencies and non-governmental organizations had collaborated in this way, and the Group remains a unique example of co-operation between international and non-governmental institutions.

SERIES TITLES – in order of scheduled publication

- **WOMEN AND THE WORLD ECONOMIC CRISIS** PREPARED BY JEANNE VICKERS

- **WOMEN AND DISABILITY** PREPARED BY ESTHER R. BOYLAN

- **WOMEN AND HEALTH** PREPARED BY PATRICIA SMYKE

- **WOMEN AND THE ENVIRONMENT** PREPARED BY ANNABEL RODDA

- **REFUGEE WOMEN** PREPARED BY SUSAN FORBES MARTIN

- **WOMEN AND LITERACY** PREPARED BY MARCELA BALLARA

- **WOMEN AND THE FAMILY** PREPARED BY HELEN O'CONNELL

- **WOMEN AND WORK** PREPARED BY SUSAN BULLOCK

- **WOMEN AND EMPOWERMENT: Participation and decision-making** PREPARED BY MARILEE KARL

For full details, as well as order forms, please write to:
ZED BOOKS LTD, 7 CYNTHIA STREET, LONDON N1 9JF, U.K. and 165 First Avenue, Atlantic Highlands, New Jersey 07716, U.S.A.

WOMEN
AND WORK

PREPARED BY SUSAN BULLOCK

Zed Books Ltd · London & New Jersey

Women and Work was first published by Zed Books Ltd, 7 Cynthia Street, London N1 9JF, United Kingdom and 165 First Avenue, Atlantic Highlands, New Jersey 07716, United States of America, in 1994.

The views in this publication do not necessarily reflect the views of the United Nations.

Cover and book design by Lee Robinson
Cover Photo: J. Maillard
Typeset by Action Typesetting Limited, Gloucester
Printed and bound in the United Kingdom at The Bath Press, Avon.

British Library Cataloguing in Publication Data

A catalogue record for this book is available from the British Library

ISBN 1 85649 117 X
ISBN 1 85649 118 8

Library of Congress Cataloging-in Publication Data

A catalog record for this book is available from the US Library of Congress

CONTENTS

ACKNOWLEDGEMENTS

This book has been prepared by Susan Bullock on behalf of the Joint UN-NGO Group on Women and Development and made possible through financial contributions from:

- The Dutch Ministry of Foreign Affairs
- International Labour Organization (ILO)
- United Nations Children's Fund (UNICEF)
- United Nations Fund for Women (UNIFEM)
- International Federation of Plantation and Allied Agricultural Workers (IFPAAW)
- International Federation of Building and Wood Workers
- Public Service International (PSI)
- International Federation of Commercial, Clerical, Professional and Technical Employees

The content of this book has been approved by the UN-NGO Group on Women and Development. The following organizations have made a special contribution through their participation in the editorial panel formed for this publication:

- International Labour Organization (ILO)
- United Nations Food and Agricultural Organization (FAO)
- United Nations Industrial Development Organization (UNIDO)
- United Nations University/World Institute for Development Economics Research (UNU/WIDER)
- International Trade Centre (ITC)
- International Federation of Plantation and Allied Agricultural Workers (IFPAAW)
- Women's International League for Peace and Freedom
- Zonta International
- International Union of Food and Allied Workers Association
- International Council on Social Welfare (ICSW)
- American Association of Retired Persons (AAPR)
- International Organization of Consumers Unions (IOCU)
- International Council of Women (ICW)
- International Federation of University Women (ICJW)
- International Council of Jewish Women
- International Federation of Building and Wood Workers
- International Federation of Business and Professional Women (IFBPW)

Overall coordination and management of the UN-NGO Group on Women and Development is provided by the United Nations Non-Governmental Liaison Service (NGLS), an inter-agency unit which fosters dialogue and cooperation between the United Nations system and the NGO community on development policy issues and North-South relations.

INTRODUCTION:

FULL MEMBERS OF THE HUMAN RACE

WITHIN THE BROADER OBJECTIVE of the Women and World Development Series – to bring women's concerns more fully into the development process – this book aims to highlight the ideology and structures that limit and undervalue women's participation in the world of work and to show the action being taken, principally by women themselves, to analyse and overcome their subordination. This volume will therefore:

- bring research findings and case studies on women and work together with others on women and development;

- look at the factors that link women, in spite of their enormously different experiences and situations; and

- and report on responses and initiatives by women and their organizations, locally and internationally.

In recent years more and more women in the North have looked to the organizing strategies of women in the South for examples and ideas, and it is hoped that this book can be one more link in a two-way process of learning and exchange.

ASSUMPTIONS ☐ The book is based on certain assumptions, or beliefs, which are best made explicit.

The first is that there are no such things as 'women's issues' – or rather, that all issues are women's issues. Women have certain specific concerns, some related to their biological role and some to their lack of rights, but they also share the concerns of all citizens.

Second, and linked, is that although a gender-specific analysis is necessary in order to tackle the many faces of inequality, the target is full membership of the human race for women, as for men.

Although most of the discussion is in the context of poverty, another assumption is that neither full development nor gender symmetry has been achieved in the industrialized countries, and that although poverty is more relative than absolute in the North, it is a reality for those who experience it, and a condition suffered by increasing numbers of people.

STRUCTURE OF THIS BOOK ☐ Chapter 1 introduces some of the ideas that will be part of later, more detailed discussion – in particular the concept of gender and how it relates both to work and to development.

Chapter 2 provides an overview of some trends in employment generally, and women's employment in particular, and discusses some of the main issues that affect women's productive and reproductive work.

The next three chapters present women in different situations and conditions of work. Chapter 3 looks at the role of women in agriculture and other rural activities, Chapter 4 at the informal sector, Chapter 5 at the way women have been brought into the global labour force, and at the impact of industrialization.

Chapter 6 raises questions about the positive and negative effects of schooling and further training, while Chapter 7 examines international labour standards, and other measures that have been taken to promote equal opportunities and treatment at work.

Finally, Chapter 8 considers the ways in which a combination of grassroots organization – from trade unions to women's own groups – and international action can strengthen the power of women in order to secure their rights and bring about social change.

LIMITATIONS ☐ The ground this book attempts to cover is extensive, as work touches every facet of human life. Among the consequences three, in particular, are acknowledged: the first is that it has been difficult to avoid making generalizations, despite the fact that the tendency to generalize about women has been unhelpful, to say the least, in view of the important differences between them in their specific historical, cultural, ethnic and class situations. Second, for the sake of clarity and ease of presentation, the book is divided into chapters which imply a demarcation between sectors and issues which does not exist in reality. Third, this book has attempted to introduce and summarize a great number of complex concepts and debates, and in so doing has drawn on the committed work of many people, which although acknowledged is not done justice to for reasons of space. Readers are encouraged to take up some of the references in order to gain fuller information and follow through some analyses in greater depth.

TERMINOLOGY ☐ All discussions about development are immediately confronted with the problem of finding the right words to describe certain regions of the world and the relationship between them. For the sake of variety, a number of alternatives are used in this text, although all have their limitations. A glossary of terms and abbreviations is provided in Annex I.

Fisher girl, El Salvador

WOMEN, WORK AND DEVELOPMENT

Half the world stock of intelligence is female, and half the world's human resources are embodied by women.... It will take male and female thinking, experience and effort to fashion a new and better world. In the meeting of men and women on equal terms, a new dynamism and creativity can be developed.

BÖRJE HORNLUND, SWEDISH MINISTER OF LABOUR[1]

WORK IS A BASIC ELEMENT of our common humanity. We all work – though we may not be recognized and waged – and work underpins the struggle for development. It is the wasted potential of so many people, who are willing to undertake the tasks society needs to be done but who are prevented from doing so by an uneven distribution of power and resources, which enables underdevelopment to persist.

WOMEN, WORK AND DEVELOPMENT

□ Women have always worked, and their labour 'plays a key role in the survival of millions of families'.[2] They work longer hours than men and have a greater range of responsibilities, but the work they do is often neither publicly nor privately acknowledged. Women are not a minority group or special category and, similarly, women's work is not just another issue. Although women have been subordinated and marginalized in different ways for much of history, their labour – and the exploitation of that labour – is the foundation of society's wealth. Women perform the vital function of producing society's producers, and yet this role is made to appear private, marginal, and without economic value. What are the structures that keep men and women in separate spheres, and ensure that the spheres of men are dominant and of women subordinate?

GENDER RELATIONS

□ Gender is the term used to describe the relations between men and women that, although based on biological differences, are socially and culturally created. For example, although the biological fact of having a child does not, in itself, make it impossible for a woman to have a job, she may be prevented by a number of factors determined by gender: among them cultural norms restricting women to the home, stereotypes about 'suitable' jobs for women, or the lack of child care and family services. In spite of the different degrees and forms of gender inequality, the system is universal. Women have in common the multiple activities they are expected to carry out, while their 'official' sphere is the home and family. The extent of female disadvantage, and the forms it takes, may vary but what remains constant is that women have seldom been more advantaged than men in any society.

Gender structures social, political and economic relations, and shapes values and attitudes throughout society. An important aspect of gender-based analysis is that it moves away from 'women's issues' to considering structures that affect and are affected by both men and women. Explanations of the origins of gender include anthropological, psychoanalytical, and economic analyses among many others. What is important is to see gender as a social construction and not a law of nature. This means that it can be challenged and, ultimately, transformed. As Valentine Moghadam says:

[G]ender systems ... may be affected by changes in production and distribution, and changes in

1

consciousness and political forces.... Changes may be unintentional, with unintended consequences, or deliberate, the result of specific policies and political interventions.[3]

THE SEXUAL DIVISION OF LABOUR The division between production – paid work or 'economic activity' – and reproduction – the bearing and care of children plus the general management of the household – is the basis of what is known as the sexual division of labour. Reproduction may be considered to include the maintenance of community as well as family life. A division exists not only between domestic and pro-

ductive work, but also within each category. The fact that women's primary role is reproduction helps explain why women's jobs cover a narrower range of activities than men's and echo women's reproductive responsibilities: service jobs, in particular, such as cleaning, caring, teaching and food processing.

Pay tends to be low in occupations dominated by women because of their association with the domestic sphere, and because women are still widely considered to be 'secondary' wage earners. Women are also paid less because they are seen as unskilled. In a study of changing structures

Women's jobs echo their responsibilities: a hotel maid in the USA

PHOTO: ILO/J. MAILLARD

in employment, the Organisation for Economic Co-operation and Development (OECD) states:

Many of the skills actually required in female occupations are not reflected in current occupational definitions or job descriptions. Informally acquired skills – 'tacit' skills – tend to be ignored even when they are essential for the task at hand.[4]

The sexual division of labour also applies to the organization of the household. Studies that reveal the dynamics of bargaining, decision-making, and gender relations within the household have made an important contribution to our understanding of both production and consumption. We learn that the household is not a homogeneous unit but, as Amartya Sen calls it, a scene of 'cooperative conflict',[5] where there are different interests, expectations, contributions, needs, and degrees of control. In *Gender and Development: Practical Guidelines*, Kate Young examines concepts and practicalities relating to household resource management, and also some of the assumptions of those attempting to alleviate poverty. These assumptions include: treating the household as a unit; assuming that the male 'head of household' is the main provider; and expecting that the household income will be fairly divided.[6] The weaker bargaining position of women – wives and daughters – is demonstrated in many ways including the poorer health and nutrition of women and girls, and their lower levels of schooling. Most accounts of expenditure emphasize the very small amounts of cash that women can raise and therefore dispose of, and how little they spend on themselves, even if in need of, say, medical care.

WOMEN'S LABOUR, WOMEN'S BODIES

Production and reproduction are also linked through and in women's bodies.

Most women who work as prostitutes do so because they need income and they have no other job possibilities; women may sell sex as one of a number of survival strategies, something they turn to if they need money. Women's limited control over their sexuality and fertility demonstrates not just their poor economic opportunities but also their lack of autonomy and basic human rights.

Capitalizing on women's bodies is not confined to commercial sex work. Advertisements for many products and services make unspecified promises about the availability of women, which have nothing to do with the product in hand. Even investment is attracted on this basis: selling free trade zones (FTZs) on the basis of a workforce of young, docile girls conjures up more images than simply their lack of militancy. The assumption that women are – or should be – available to men, that their bodies are commodities like any others to be bought or appropriated, is at the root of the growing violence against women that Maria Mies calls the 'common denominator' of women's exploitation and oppression, irrespective of country, race or class.[7]

GENDER AND POWER

Gender is not, of course, the only system of oppression, and the subordination of women is linked with the subordination of other groups on the basis of race, handicap or age, and with the class system. Systems of stratification and oppression do not just resemble one other but are mutually reinforcing. They have in common the concentration of power in the hands of certain groups at the expense of others, and there is considerable overlap between groups.

Power and control are exercised in many different ways – direct and indirect – in the home, the workplace and the community. One important mechanism is culture, including religious beliefs. Culture and tradition are not only used as means of control, but also as its justification: it is not men who demand the seclusion of women, but religious faith; it is not men who wish the mutilation of women's genitalia, but customary practice; it is not men who insist that women's heads should be lower than theirs, it is the custom. Culture and religion are used to shape attitudes, dictate practice, and maintain inequality as 'the norm'.[8]

While respect for cultural diversity and heritage remains important, there is a profound difference between cultural identity and oppressive practices, however traditional. It should also be recognized that if it is in the interests of men to ignore or change a customary practice, they do so without hesitation. Many traditions, some of arguably social value, have been abandoned in the name of progress. Others are of relatively recent origin, adopted because they benefit certain groups. Many practices and ideas in Southern Africa, for example, far from being 'traditional' and of long standing, were constructed during the colonial period.[9]

GENDER AND DEVELOPMENT □ Discussion of the relationship between women, work and development, and the policy decisions and planning which affect them, needs to take place in the context of these interdependent systems of control. In 'Gender matters in development', Ruth Pearson gives us this warning:

... we can't think in terms of analysing development and then looking at its effect on women.... All policies, however technical or neutral they may appear to be, will have gendered implications.[10]

Gender-and-development (GAD) has come to replace an approach that was more narrowly focused on women alone, divorced from the social and economic systems to which they belong. GAD should be seen as building on and refining the women-in-development (WID) approach, however, rather than invalidating it. WID played a key role in bringing to public attention the extent and value of women's many activities. The work of Ester Boserup,[11] in particular, has come to be seen as a landmark; a number of activists and NGOs also raised critical questions about the theory and practice of development in the early 1970s. The women-in-development literature has addressed the work issue by insisting on the recognition and valuing of the full range of women's work: not just unpaid economic activity but also domestic tasks. Much research was stimulated by and took place in the course of the United Nations Decade for Women (see below).

In the course of establishing the scope and complexity of women's productive

WHAT WORK HAS VALUE?
In the World Council of Churches report *Women, Poverty and the Economy* Maria Riley asks: 'What would it mean if we used the work women do as the criterion to judge our present economic system? Primarily, I believe it would require us to reassess what we identify — and reward economically — as valuable work for human and societal well-being. Secondly, I suggest that it would call upon us to radically re-structure not only our economic systems but also our work patterns.

'Our economic system and our ideas of work have been shaped predominantly by men's experience, an experience which has been supported historically by a corps of invisible back-up workers.... The question should not be how to integrate women into this sphere, but how to reorganize [it] to ensure that it reflects the full complement of human work and human workers, female and male. In asking the questions from the vantage point of women's work, we begin to discern some of the outlines of the radical transformation that will be demanded when we begin to take the experience of women seriously as ... formative for our political and economic structures.'[15]

and reproductive roles, WID and then GAD have also helped to establish 'the full personhood of women'[12] in contrast with views of women as either passive victims or selfless 'channels' of development. It is increasingly recognized that the exclusion of women from social and economic participation is a violation of human rights. Self-determination is therefore a vital part of the gender-aware approach, because this means women setting the targets as well as being involved as implementers and beneficiaries.[13] Both development and the transformation of gender relations will involve the exercise of power by those systematically deprived of autonomy and control in their lives. The objective is not, however, simply the transfer of control from one group to another but to achieve a broader base for participation and access to resources.

Diane Elson sees a challenge ahead for GAD. At a seminar organized by the United Nations Division for the Advancement of Women (DAW), she argued that gender-aware development can take one of two courses: demonstrate that women can contribute to the achievement of existing plans and priorities; or, recast the development agenda on the basis of women's perceptions and priorities, making gender a central element of analysis and, in particular, developing targets and programmes that give as much importance to reproduction as to production.[14]

THE IMPACT OF MACRO POLICIES

'GAD has also started to eliminate the gap between 'women's issues' and mainstream policy, but much work remains to be done to make connections at all levels. The United Nations Research Institute for Social Development (UNRISD) points out that gender awareness has not yet been turned into a planning tool above the project or programme level, nor is there 'a sustainable dialogue between planners and those within the research community who might help them towards a gender analysis'.[16] Women organizing for change need to take into account the impact on their lives of macro-economic policies. Policy decisions taken by individual governments and international agencies can undermine even the best-laid development plans. The Director of the United Nations Development Fund for Women (UNIFEM), Sharon Capeling-Alakija, gives the following warning:

There could be trouble ahead. Consider a scenario where women are off in China [at the World Conference on Women]discussing the obstacles they face while men are in New York designing the institutions that could, in all likelihood, once again deal women out of macro-policy well into the next millennium.... In the preparations for 1995 we [must ensure that] we are developing strategies that will enable women to have a central role in these discussions.[17]

Economic concepts, negotiations and analyses appear to be objective and neutral, without special reference to men or to women but, as Diane Elson has shown, there is 'a hidden agenda that covers the process of the reproduction and maintenance of human resources'.[18] This assumes that women's labour is both elastic and without cost. Women, through their reproductive and productive activities, 'cushion' households and societies against the full effects of economic restructuring, thus relieving policy-makers of the need to take human and social costs into account. This is why the primary burden of International Monetary Fund (IMF) and World Bank structural adjustment programmes has been borne by women:

- As services are cut, or charges are imposed, women have to compensate (in providing care for the young, sick or elderly, for example).

PHOTO: IIO/J. MAILLARD

Cooking for the household, Colombia

● As incomes fall and prices rise women, the household managers, 'manage the crisis' as well – by investing time to save money, by doing without, and by taking on any job that could earn them a little income.

● The public service has been almost the only source of formal-sector employment for women in many poor countries. The enormous cuts in public spending imposed as conditions for loans have cost many women their jobs.

Economic, as well as social and political, restructuring is certainly needed but the measures taken to date have both failed to go far enough and exacted unacceptably high social and human costs. Neither women, nor their labour, are in fact 'elastic', and many are stretched to breaking point. A study of IMF and World Bank programmes in eighteen developing countries concludes that they are 'optimal for neither stabilization nor growth and income redistribution in the Third World'.[19] Restructuring has been both piecemeal and ideologically driven, but it has not addressed fundamental economic problems, such as the way the international financial system is structured, and the colossal level of debt worldwide.[20]

The driving ideology has been a belief in economic growth as the target of development, and the free market as the mechanism for achieving it. As Susan George has eloquently argued, the growth model of development neglects all those aspects of life – including women's work – that cannot be counted in the gross domestic product (GDP). While the free market system can do a number of things efficiently, it cannot provide everything a society needs nor fulfil the functions of the state.[21]

OPPORTUNITIES FOR CHANGE ☐ If an analysis of the structures of oppression – the barriers to people's participation and women's rights – is a first step, and a new approach to work and development is a second, the third must be to develop strategies for change. One challenge for women is to identify the multiple levels on which action can take place and the range of alliances that are necessary for it to be effective.

It is also important to make the most of what Valentine Moghadam calls the unintentional changes, with their unintended consequences. This is perhaps the most constructive spirit in which to approach current adjustment and restructuring: to see it as an opportunity for change for the better. Women in South Africa have done exactly that: from across the political and racial divide, they have formed a Women's National Coalition to draw up a Charter for Women's Equality. Over a period of one year, women's views will be sought and demands discovered through a massive participatory research project. This will provide not only a unique database to inform policy development and planning, but also a platform for popular education and mobilization.

Possibilities exist even in the present situation, although many steps backwards appear to have been taken both in international and industrial relations. As Diane Elson urges:

Economic crisis [should be seen by women as] ... a turning point for a whole range of social institutions and practices. Restructuring opens up new opportunities as well as closing old opportunities. Oppressed and disadvantaged groups find that change creates conditions for new forms of struggle. Trying to resist the tide of change and to preserve precrisis social relations rarely works. A more creative approach

that tries to influence the terms of restructuring, to restructure not just production but social relations, and to create new institutions and organizations of and for oppressed and disadvantaged groups may have more chance of success.[22]

The long-term impact on women and on society of increased, if still exploitative, relations with the labour market may be very significant. This will not happen by itself:

Collective organization is the vital ingredient that may move female participation in paid labour from a survival strategy to a transformation strategy.[23]

This also motivates us to build on the changes that can be observed in the position of some international institutions, for example the World Bank. The fact that the World Bank acknowledges flaws in structural adjustment programmes and is building social indicators into future packages shows that, at least, a possibility for dialogue exists. The challenge for women's organizations is to know how to take part in this dialogue, and to equip themselves to take part effectively; the challenge for the World Bank, as for other official agencies – which are meant to be representative of the interests of the people – is to hear the people, acknowledge their right to take part, and make sure that it is a real dialogue.

LANDMARKS AND ACHIEVEMENTS ☐ It is important also to bear in mind the achievements of women, sometimes in partnership with progressive men: they have been part of many struggles, not only for women's rights but for political and social justice, and they have survived many crises. While progress towards full emancipation often feels desperately slow, and the remaining barriers seem immovably entrenched, there have been profound

PHOTO: PSI

Decision-making processes: but where are the women?

changes in law, in structures and in attitudes whose full effects there has not yet been time to measure. Women's awareness – of their situation and of the possibilities for change – has never been so great, and it continues to grow through formal and informal education, information, and support networks.

THE UNITED NATIONS DECADE FOR WOMEN

The year 1975 was designated by the United Nations as International Women's Year, 'devoted to intensified action to promote equality between men and women, to ensure the full integration of women in the total development effort, and to increase women's contribution to the strengthening of world peace'.[24] In the course of the year, the United Nations General Assembly proclaimed 1976–85 the United Nations Decade for Women: Equality, Development and Peace, with

three sub-themes: employment; health; and education.

The Decade for Women deserves to be acknowledged for what it achieved in giving a voice to women from all over the world, in raising awareness among the public and politicians, and in helping the development of strategies for action. Although it was undermined by economic crises in the developing countries, the Decade for Women helped to create a momentum that has not been lost. At the closing World Women's Conference in Nairobi in 1985, representatives of 157 countries agreed to endorse and adopt the Forward-looking Strategies (FLS) for the Advancement of Women. These included an undertaking to ratify and implement the United Nations Convention on the Elimination of all Forms of Discrimination against Women.

The FLS are interesting, and still relevant, for their analysis as well as their practical recommendations. They attack the assumptions that economic growth automatically benefits women, and that the needs of women can be met by welfare services. The FLS link the empowerment of women to their economic participation. The section on employment stresses a woman's right to economic independence and self-reliance through equal employ

MILESTONES ON THE ROAD TO EQUALITY

1945 The United Nations Charter enshrines the principle of equal rights for all 'without distinction as to race, sex, language or religion' (Article 1).

1946 The Commission on the Status of Women is set up by the United Nations.

1952 The Commission initiates the Convention on the Political Rights of Women – the first global mandate to grant women the legal right to vote and hold office.

1967 Declaration on the Elimination of Discrimination against Women.

1975 International Women's Year; the First World Conference on Women is held in Mexico City; 1976–85 is declared United Nations Decade for Women.

1979 The United Nations General Assembly adopts the Convention on the Elimination of all Forms of Discrimination against Women.

1980 The Second World Conference on Women is held in Copenhagen; it adopts a Programme of Action for the second half of the decade.

1982 The first meeting takes place of the Committee on the Elimination of Discrimination against Women (CEDAW), set up to monitor compliance with the Convention

on the Elimination of all Forms of Discrimination against Women.

1985 The Third World Conference on Women, held in Nairobi, reviews progress during the United Nations Decade for Women and adopts the Forward-looking Strategies for the Advancement of Women.

1990 The Commission on the Status of Women undertakes a five-year review of progress on the implementation of the Forward-looking Strategies.

1994 Five regional conferences take place to prepare for Beijing.

1995 Fourth World Conference on Women to be held in Beijing.

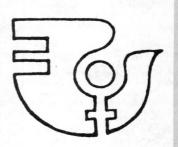

**International
Women's Day**

ment opportunities. The FLS emphasize the key role of trade unions, and also urge action by governments:

[Governments should work with] international and regional organisations, and NGOs ... to enhance the self-reliance of women in a viable and sustained fashion .... Grassroots participatory processes, and planning approaches using local ... expertise and resources, are vital and should be supported.[25]

An institution that had been dismissed by some as too remote, bureaucratic and official made it possible for women from vastly different backgrounds and experiences to meet. These women not only conveyed their priorities to the United Nations, but actually changed the priorities of this unwieldy institution and its agencies. The lesson that can be drawn from this is never to dismiss any potential ally, but to work at every level, in every sector, using every means at our disposal so long as

we retain a clear vision of our objectives.

LOOKING AHEAD: BEIJING, 1995

The Fourth World Conference on Women, to be held in Beijing in 1995, will examine the new report on the state of the world's women, evaluate progress so far in implementing the FLS, and work out a new programme of action. What is essential is that women do not continue to be marginalized. Following 1985, governments and international agencies set up women's bureaux, divisions, commissions and funds, almost all of which were under-resourced, under-staffed, and – most important – outside the mainstream planning and decision-making processes. The 1995 conference must resist the temptation simply to describe, even to analyse, women's experience of oppression and the barriers to equality: the focus must be on moving forward, both conceptually, in terms of targets, and practically, in terms of strategies.

1. Provisional record, Twentieth Sitting of the Eightieth Session of the International Labour Conference, 16 June 1993.
2. Editorial in *Women and Development*, double issue of *INSTRAW News*, No. 16 (1991), p. 14.
3. Valentine Moghadam, *Gender, Development and Policy: Toward Equity and Empowerment*, United Nations University (UNU WIDER) World Institute for Development Economics Research, Helsinki, 1991, pp. 9–10.
4. Organisation for Economic Co-operation and Development, *Shaping Structural Change: the Role of Women*, OECD, Paris, 1991, p. 19.
5. Kate Young, 'Household resource management', quoting from A. Sen, *Gender and Cooperative Conflicts* in Lise Østergaard (ed.), *Gender and Development: Practical Guidelines*, Routledge, London and New York, 1992, p. 155.
6. Ibid., p. 154.
7. Maria Mies, *Patriarchy and Accumulation on a World Scale*, Zed Books, London, 1986, p. 170.
8. This discussion is developed in Marilee Karl, *Women and Empowerment* (Women and World Development Series), Zed Books, London, 1994.
9. Anne Akeroyd, 'Gender, food production and property rights', in Haleh Afshar (ed.), *Women, Development and Survival in the Third World*, Longman, Harlow, 1991, p. 146.
10. Ruth Pearson, 'Gender matters in development', in T. Allen and A.Thomas (eds), *Poverty and Development in the 1990s*, Oxford University Press, Oxford, 1993, p. 292.
11. Ester Boserup, *Women's Role in Economic Development*, St Martin's Press, New York, 1970.
12. Georgina Ashworth, *Women and Human Rights*, background paper for the OECD/DAC Expert Group on Women in Development, Change, London, 1992, p. 15.
13. Jan Pronk, 'Advancing towards autonomy', speech to Women in Development seminar, The Hague, 13 June 1991.
14. Diane Elson, 'Gender issues in development strategies', paper prepared for the seminar on the Integration of Women in Development, United Nations Division for the Advancement of Women, Vienna, 1991.
15. Maria Riley, 'Women and work: linking faith and justice', in *Women, Poverty and the Economy*, World Council of Churches, Geneva, 1988, p. 7.
16. UNRISD is currently undertaking a project to strengthen the capacity of countries to integrate gender into development policy. See Progress Report by the Director, UNRISD, Geneva, 1993.
17. 'The United Nations and women', *INSTRAW News*, No. 18, 1992.
18. Diane Elson, 'From survival strategies to transformation strategies: women's needs and structural adjustment', in Lourdes Benería and Shelley Feldman (eds), *Unequal Burden: Economic Crises, Persistent Poverty, and Women's Work*, Westview Press, Boulder and Oxford, 1992, p. 34.
19. Lance Taylor, *Varieties of Stabilization Experience*, Clarendon Press, Oxford, 1988.
20. Elson, 'From survival strategies'.

21. Susan George, 'A war against the poor', *PSI Focus*, No. 8, 1993.

22. Elson, 'From survival strategies', p. 29.

23. Ibid., p. 40.

24. United Nations, *The Nairobi Forward-looking Strategies for the Advancement of Women*, United Nations Department of Public Information, New York, 1986, paragraph 2.

25. Ibid., paragraph 113.

2 WOMEN WORKING WORLDWIDE

If women were paid for all they do
There'd be a lot of wages due …

Written on a China money box, made in the shape of a rolling pin, England, 1940s[1]

When we look at categories and statistics of work, we have to ask what is being counted as work. For many years, in many societies, only work outside the home – productive work – has counted as 'real' work. As it is also linked to pay or income, official statistics often refer to numbers of people in 'economic activity'.

But what about the many tasks carried out by women in and near the home? 'One common criticism of the economic activity concept is that the work many women do, ostensibly outside the labour force, such as walking long distances in rural areas to fetch water, is of as much use-value as being economically active in the more conventional sense.'[2] This is why women's work is sometimes called 'invisible' – but it is invisible only to statisticians, planners and policy-makers. It is in fact very hard not to see the work women do. The stories of Kham and Marie, right, highlight this point.

These women's routines show how production and reproduction overlap: Kham and Marie, and millions of women, do both productive and reproductive work, and sometimes it is hard to see where one ends and the other begins. But there is another link: their reproductive

KHAM AND MARIE

Khamsaphone gets up at five o'clock and goes out to fetch wood from a copse near the village. She returns, lights her stove, makes tea with some dried herbs, then steams sticky rice for the day's meals. The children go to school, except her eldest daughter whose help she needs that day. They sit together to mend two home-made fishing nets and then they go to one of the ponds that have appeared since the start of the rainy season. They catch a few small fish which they later put out to dry. Kham takes rice to the field where her husband is working and is told that in two days' time she will be needed for transplanting. At home again, she goes to the well to fill the stone storage jars, washes the school shirts of her sons, then prepares a basket of rice to take to the monks in the temple. She cooks, serves and cleans after the evening meal, and prepares a fish and chili sauce for the next day. She goes to bed at ten o'clock.

Marie gets up at six o'clock, makes packed lunches for her husband and two children, irons some clothes, prepares breakfast, then wakes the family and dresses her youngest child. He has a cough, but she can't keep him off school as there's no one to look after him. She hurries to work at a hairdressing salon, where she is on her feet most of the day. She does the shopping in her lunch break. When she gets home in the afternoon, she prepares the evening meal, and cleans the kitchen and bathroom. She helps the older children with their homework, and tots up the household accounts for the week. After eating, she washes up, puts some laundry into the washing machine, watches television for half an hour, then goes to bed.

work in fact contributes to production. By their labour, both are subsidizing the production and maintenance of the workforce. Because women 'labour for love', society in general and employers in particular are saved the expense of the upkeep of the workforce, either in terms of providing communal services – canteens, child care, laundries – or in terms of paying wages high enough to cover the real costs. Their 'non-productive' work in fact makes an enormous economic contribution.

12

The concept of 'economic activity' is therefore criticized not only for its limitations, but also because it encourages the non-recognition of women's multiple activities and, in effect, institutionalizes the unequal relations between men and women. What is needed is to find ways of recognizing and valuing not only the economic contribution of women, but also their social contribution: the care, sustenance and support given by women to their families, households, and communities.

WOMEN COUNT ☐ It is true, however, that the nature and scope of women's work is no longer a neglected area. Issues that have been addressed include the absence of separate employment and unemployment statistics for women and men; the use of occupational categories that obscure the range of women's activities and skills; and the insensitivity of analysts to different interpretations of economic activity and to cultural, regional and seasonal variations.[3] Particular attention has been given to the undercounting of female economic activity, and to the lack of mechanisms for counting women's unpaid labour: be it in family businesses and farms, 'informal' activities, or domestic work. As a consequence, steps have been taken to broaden the concept of work and to devise methodologies for measuring it more accurately and comprehensively. These include: an International Labour Organisation (ILO) convention on labour statistics (1985); revisions to the International Standard Classification of Occupations (ISCO); and efforts by the United Nations Food and Agricultural Organization (FAO) to change the guidelines for the World Programme of Agricultural Censuses.

Time-use statistics can be useful

The multiple roles of women: a mother in Bolivia

PHOTO: UNICEF/A. GRACIANO

UNIFEM joined forces with the United Nations Population Fund (UNFPA) to ensure that when India's national census took place in 1991, women would get a fairer representation. Seminars and meetings took place to sensitize statisticians and government officials to gender issues, and a public information campaign was conducted.

The Sisterhood is Global Institute has a census project which has been taken up by a range of women's organizations in different countries; this aims to make women's unpaid labour visible in national censuses, based on time-use principles below.

One of the achievements of The World's Women: Trends and Statistics 1970–1990 (a joint initiative by the United Nations Statistical Office, the United Nations Children's Fund (UNICEF), UNFPA and UNIFEM) is to present statistics about women that do cover many of their multiple roles. This comprehensive and interesting report covers women and the environment, health, education, families, and public life as well as economic activity. It also highlights the area of women's unpaid work, its extent and its value.

because they move away from the vexed questions of economic contribution and occupational categories, and look at what people actually do: they measure time spent on all activities, productive and reproductive, and the classifications used are not based on occupational groupings. Studies that are derived from this approach have often enabled researchers and analysts to challenge official employment figures and narrow definitions of work. They have shown that, worldwide, women work longer hours than men, apart from in Australia and North America where the hours turn out to be roughly even. Efforts are now being made to improve the methodology: it has been recognized that it lacks precision in breaking down different activities, and that underestimation persists both of time spent and of the range of tasks undertaken.

MORE WOMEN WORKING ☐ Many of the reforms and revisions outlined above are only just starting to have an impact on the collection of information at national level, so the figures that follow suffer from the limitations already described, most particularly the underestimation of female economic activity.

Three-quarters of the 5,300 million people on the earth (1990) live in the developing regions. Just under half of them are women. Some 55 per cent of the world's women live in Asia and the Pacific, 12.5 per cent live in Africa, 8.5 per cent live in Latin America and the Caribbean, and 23.5 per cent live in the industrialized regions (including the former socialist states).[4]

More women are in paid and self-employment than ever before. According to official measurements, 41 per cent of the world's women aged fifteen and over are economically active, though using different criteria this number could be double. Between 1970 and 1990 women's share in the labour force increased in many but not all regions: it remained constant at fairly high levels in Southeast and East Asia, and actually declined in sub-Saharan Africa. The increase was greatest in North America – from 33 to 41 per cent – and high in the other OECD countries.[5] The year 1990 also saw the beginning of what may be a substantial decline in the high numbers of economically active women in central and eastern Europe.

The United Nations study *The World's Women* points out that growth in the female labour force has been undermined by economic recession in most developing countries and many of the developed.

Women generally continue to be the last to benefit from job expansion and the first to suffer from job contraction – particularly in the stagnant or declining economies of Africa and Latin Amer-

Table 2.1: WOMEN'S SHARE IN THE LABOUR FORCE 1970 AND 1990

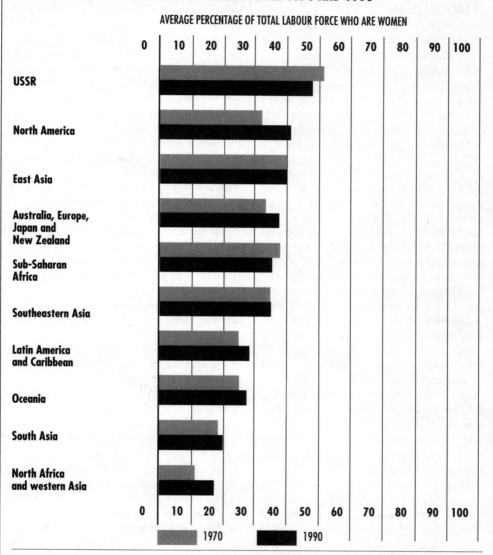

AVERAGE PERCENTAGE OF TOTAL LABOUR FORCE WHO ARE WOMEN

■ 1970 ■ 1990

SOURCE: *THE WORLD'S WOMEN: TRENDS AND STATISTICS, 1970–1990*, UNITED NATIONS, NEW YORK, 1991.

ica and the Caribbean. In Africa, due to especially severe economic conditions, the growth in the female labour force has fallen well behind population growth.[6]

In Benin, for example, where women make up only 6 per cent of workers in the formal sector, the proportion of women retrenched from the public service was 21 per cent.[7] Although the proportion of economically active men is also declining, the gaps between women's recorded participation and men's remain wide in all regions.

15

TRENDS AND FACTORS IN WOMEN'S EMPLOYMENT □

Why do women work? The answer is put succinctly in the *World Labour Report*: 'Many [women] want to work – and now exercise a freedom denied to previous generations. Others are forced to work to survive.'[8] The rise in women's participation in the labour force has been the result of these two, sometimes overlapping, factors: a greater choice open to women, and more pressure on them to ensure the maintenance or survival of their families. The third factor is the need of economies for a type of labour women can provide. Although most women have to bring in an income, a job can be more than mere drudgery and survival. Many women, and not only in better-paid and professional occupations, have gained a sense of worth and self-confidence through their work. However, the reasons for and rewards from work vary enormously between industrialized and developing regions, and between classes, ethnic and age groups. So do the ways in which women have been absorbed into wage labour, although they have in common the fact that they have generally entered on less advantageous terms than men.

In most industrialized countries, despite women's intense economic activity in certain regions and sectors – the textile industry, farming and domestic service, for example – opportunities for women in general were restricted until the Second World War and the two decades of rapid economic growth that followed. At the same time, women's own possibilities were increased and their expectations were raised as a result of higher education levels, greater control over fertility, availability of convenience foods and domestic gadgets, and changing social attitudes. The expansion both in services and in part-time employment matched women's needs and experience, and this also encouraged their participation. The pattern of working life has changed over time: before the 1950s, most women workers were young and unmarried; a second group were women whose children had grown up and left home. Economic activity is now becoming more continuous – that is, with fewer, and shorter, breaks for raising a family – and it is no longer unusual (or illegal) for married women to be employed.

In developing countries, industrialization tends to coexist with agriculture, rather than displacing it, and family businesses – from farms to small enterprises – have been and remain important employers of women. There has, therefore, been not so much a movement of women 'into the labour force' as changes in the nature of women's work, except in some of the rapidly industrializing Asian countries. The changes have often involved a move from subsistence farming or other unpaid activity to labouring or informal income generation. A working life has always been longer, and more continuous, for most women in developing countries: girls may give substantial help in the home, be unpaid family workers or even wage earners; women – especially in rural areas – hardly interrupt their work routine to have a baby, and they keep working until the end of their lives.

At the same time, pressure has increased on women everywhere to make up or provide the family wage. A vicious circle of debt, inflation, economic stagnation and unemployment has increased the numbers of the poor, and has placed the heaviest burden on women. As prices rise and incomes fall, women increase their working hours and diversify their activities to ensure the family's survival – in rich countries as well as poor. The 'feminization of poverty' is an abstract-sounding term which means that more and more women are poor, and more of the poor are women.

PHOTO: ILO/J. MAILLARD

More women in employment than ever before: a fish-packing plant in Thailand

THE CHANGING SHAPE OF FAMILIES

The family is contracting in many parts of the world: although multi-generation families remain common in developing countries, they are becoming 'narrower', with fewer adult siblings living in the same household. In most regions, fewer children are being born too. The increase in life expectancy, and a healthy life expectancy, means that societies have a rising proportion of older people. Many live with their children, but an increasing number have independent households. Another factor that is having an increasingly severe impact on households and whole communities is incapacity and death resulting from infection by the HIV virus, which causes AIDS. Because those principally affected are adults in the prime of life, children are losing parents and households their most productive members. Women are bearing much of the responsibility for care; they are also being infected more rapidly than men. In Africa, for example, where two-thirds of total infections are currently found, the numbers of women with the virus are believed to exceed those of men.

WOMEN-HEADED HOUSEHOLDS

More and more women are finding themselves the only adult in the household. In all regions the numbers of female-headed households are rising, and in most they exceed 20 per cent. The average in much of sub-Saharan Africa and the Caribbean is 30 per cent; it is 25 per cent in the developed regions, and over 20 per cent in Southeast Asia and Latin America.[9] One part of the downward spiral of poverty is the breaking up of families and households. Growing poverty can cause the disintegration of families – family members leave, temporarily or permanently, to seek better opportunities. At the same time, the reduction in the number of adults – and perhaps the absence of men – results in further poverty. Rising life expectancy for women, in particular, means that there are many elderly women living alone, especially in the developed regions. In rural areas, women heading households are often doubly penalized – they are deprived of the man's physical labour, but do not have the full legal rights and access to credit and services that most men would have. Women-headed households are overrepresented among the poor of rural and urban, developing and indus-trialized societies.

MIGRATION Migration is as old as time, but also a distinctive feature of the latter part of the twentieth century. Patterns of migration, the motivation for and condi-tions of migration, all vary considerably although most people are driven by the desire, or need, to find better opportuni-ties. They may perceive these to exist in a nearby town, a far-off city, a neighbouring country, or the other side of the world. In some situations those who migrate have a certain level of resources: information, money for the journey, perhaps some-where to stay, and initiative. Others, how-ever, migrate because the household simply cannot sustain all its members: one who leaves – even with nothing to go to – is one less mouth to feed. Seasonal migra-tion takes place mainly within the rural areas or, increasingly, is an option taken up by some urban dwellers who go to their rural home areas during the harvest season.[10]

More women than men are moving from the countryside to the city, except in Africa. Women have outnumbered men in rural–urban migration since the 1960s in Latin America and since the 1970s in Asia.[11] The great majority of migrants are under the age of twenty-five, and 40 per cent are under fifteen. Many of this youngest group are girls – not only in Latin America but also in some African and Asian countries.[12] Most go into domestic service, and a number are single mothers. There is also a significant group of women who move in their late fifties and sixties, unlike men of the same age. Most are sepa-rated, divorced or widowed.

International migration frequently takes place within a region: from Mexico to the United States, for example, or from south-ern to northern and western Europe. Two of the most important flows of migrants at present are from eastern Europe west-wards, and from Southeast Asia east-wards.[13] This form of migration has been associated with the young, single male, but nearly half of all international migrants are female. Nor do most of them go as depen-dants of a man; seven out of ten women move in search of a job and not for family reasons.[14] When migration becomes a necessity, because of war or famine, for example, those who are displaced are con-sidered to be refugees rather than migrants. Women and children represent about three-quarters of the world's refugees (for further information, see *Refugee Women* by Susan Forbes Martin in this series).

Some local economies are subsidized by remittances sent from overseas, or from the city, but very often those left behind have difficulty in managing without the labour or financial contribution of those who have left, especially when the migrant is the male head of household. Surveys show that although women generally earn less than men, they send money home more regularly; they also send a larger share of their income.[15]

UNEMPLOYMENT The final decades of the twentieth century have been marked by a widespread though fluctuating rise in unemployment in both industrialized and developing regions. Job creation has not kept pace with the increase in population, even at times of economic expansion. This has been a 'push' factor in migration, one reason for the growth of the informal sector, and at the root of the rise in poverty. It is significant that governments – and society at large – seem prepared to tol-

The International Convention on the Protection of the Rights of Migrant Workers and Members of their Families was approved by the United Nations General Assembly in 1990. It has not yet, however, been ratified by enough states to enable it to enter into force.

erate ever-higher levels of unemployment. The growth in non-standard employment has become a form of compensation: women's part-time jobs or women's informal activities are used to take the edge off the impact of male unemployment. This is not an acceptable policy response.

Women are overrepresented among the unemployed in many countries, although official figures certainly underestimate the extent of women's unemployment. The numbers of young people without jobs, and of the long-term unemployed, are very worrying. The European OECD countries have seen a steady rise in unemployment since the mid-1970s, with persistently high levels even at times of economic growth. In spite of the increased number of women in paid employment in this region, more women are also registering as unemployed. 'This apparent paradox reflects the high levels of hidden reserves of labour [among] women.'[16] That is to say, despite the enormous increase in numbers of women in the labour force, still more women are trying to get paid work. In central and eastern Europe, where unemployment is rising sharply, female unemployment is higher than male in all countries except Hungary.

UNDEREMPLOYED AND UNDERUSED

Unemployment statistics are sometimes hard to obtain for developing countries, and they are often not broken down by gender. In any case, unemployment is a concept of little relevance to the majority of rural workers, and to many urban workers too. Problems of pay and productivity have a much greater impact on their lives. Most women in the urban areas of developing countries do not even register as unemployed but look to the informal sector for income. Here and in the rural areas women are, if anything, *over*employed even if *under*paid. Women's domestic work obligations severely restrict the time they have available for income-generating work. The

ILO study *Women in the World of Work* broadens the concept of unemployment to include underemployment and underutilization:

The underemployed are those who would like additional work, who work for low incomes or whose skills are underutilized. Underemployment is most characteristic of developing countries where large numbers of people are engaged in involuntary part-time work, seasonal activity or full-time work at low pay.... In many parts of the world women's labour is underutilized; of particular concern are those who are not looking for work because there is no work suitable for them or who have become discouraged because they are the victims of prejudice.[17]

WORK AND AGE Older women are overrepresented among those whose labour is underutilized. Women are in any case the victims of stereotypical views about their capabilities and rightful 'sphere', and older women even more so. Discrimination against older women can force them into unwanted and unnecessary inactivity. This can be particularly frustrating to women whose careers may only have started, or restarted, in their forties following the raising of a family.

What is old? In Western societies an artificial cutoff point has established itself at around sixty, a common age for retirement. In most other societies, working life is a continuum which rarely breaks either for child-rearing or 'retirement'. Life expectancy is rising everywhere. The number of people aged sixty-five and over was estimated to be 328 million in 1990, and projected to reach 828 million in 2025: an increase of just over 6 per cent of the world's population to almost 10 per cent.[18] It is therefore essential that older people come to be seen as an asset and not a problem. As women age, their freedom from the ties of young children increases their mobility, and the experience they have gained in the performance of their multiple roles is of both social and economic value. While the contribution of women in general is starting to be better appreciated, that of older women remains greatly underestimated.

Women have different needs in terms of training and employment at different stages of their lives, and it would be helpful to women at all stages if both training and employment were less compartmentalized and more of a continuum. Old age should be seen as one of these stages, not as outside the productive process. Well-planned education, training and retraining throughout a lifetime, plus special savings schemes, are among the ways women could be helped to prepare for and get more from their later years, retaining a degree of self-reliance. Savings pro-

For most women, there is no retirement

PHOTO: ILO/J. MAILLARD

grammes could also be linked to credit schemes, so that older women had access to credit as well as training.[19] Nevertheless, certain factors mean that women's vulnerability increases as they age: older women are more likely to live in poverty than are older men or younger women; the chances of ill-health or reduced mobility grow with age; and changes in family structures mean that less care may be available to older family members who need it. The other side of the coin from promoting the independence and participation of older women is the provision of medical and social services that can respond to their particular needs.

PART-TIME WORKING Part-time work may be an example of underemployment, a response to unemployment, or an indirect form of exploitation. It may also fulfil a particular function in an individual's life cycle: it can be a stepping stone to full-time employment for young people, a help for workers with family responsibilities, and an option for older workers or those wishing to pursue an educational or leisure activity. Many women are forced into part-time work as the only way to combine a job with their domestic responsibilities. This is also true outside formal sector employment: millions of poor women have limited opportunities to increase their incomes because of their heavy domestic tasks and lack of access to services or technology that might relieve their burden.

Relatively rare in Asia and Africa, part-time employment has grown substantially in all industrialized countries except the United States, and in parts of Latin America. Between 1983 and 1987, 70 per cent of all jobs created in the European Community were part-time, as were over half of those created in Australia, New Zealand, and Japan.[20] In all countries, the majority of part-time workers are women, although there is a clear trend in most OECD coun-

tries for the numbers of men in part-time work (as a proportion of all male employees) to rise.[21] The greatest concentration of part-time working is in the service sector.

The danger is that part-time workers lose out compared with full-timers: pay rates may be lower, and benefits – from maternity leave to pensions – may be denied to them. More part-time than full-time contracts are casual, temporary or otherwise precarious. An important variable is the number of hours worked; below a certain threshold workers may have access to few rights under the law.

In addition, part-time working is often seen as being incompatible with a 'career', so training and promotion opportunities are rare. Part-time workers are also less likely to be unionized than full-time workers, but changes in attitude to part-time working as it has become better established, changes in union strategy, and changes in the law have combined to improve the terms and conditions of substantial numbers of part-timers.

The increase in part-time working has been so widespread, especially in the industrialized countries, that it is questionable whether we should still regard it as 'non-standard' employment. It seems likely that, before long, part-time work will be seen less as second-best than as an option with many advantages, providing that it commands a fair wage and terms of employment. The ILO considered a special report on this issue at the 1993 International Labour Conference, covering both measures for the protection of the rights of part-time workers and ways to promote part-time working.[22] The way has been paved for the adoption in 1994 of an international standard on part-time working.

WHAT WOMEN DO □ There have been enormous shifts of labour across sectors in the last few decades. Employment in agriculture has declined everywhere – slowly in Africa and most parts of Asia, considerably in the developed regions and Latin America. Manufacturing has also declined in the old industrialized countries, while it has grown in the new ones. Services have been the main growth area in the developed regions and Latin America, and are gaining in importance in Asia.

LESS DEVELOPED REGIONS Most women still work in the rural areas in much of Asia and Africa. Nearly 80 per cent of economically active women in sub-Saharan Africa, and at least half in most parts of Asia except the Middle East, are in agriculture and related activities. The numbers are much lower for Latin America and the Caribbean, but here substantial underreporting appears to take place in the official statistics. Quite substantial changes have taken place over time: in 1950, 87 per cent of economically active women in developing countries were in agriculture, as well as 78 per cent of men. By 1980, the proportion was 71 per cent of women and 63 per cent of men. The FAO projects that by the year 2000 only 57 per cent of women and 51 per cent of men will be working in agriculture.[23] The United Nations Statistical Office, however, reported little decline in the numbers of women in agriculture between 1970 and 1980, and although urbanization is continuing – especially in Latin America – rural populations are also increasing in Africa and Asia.

Women make up under 30 per cent of the workers in industry and services. The regional differences are considerable: services provide employment for 71 per cent of economically active women in Latin America and the Caribbean, for 40 per cent in Asia and the Pacific, but for only 20 per cent in Africa. More than half the economically active women in sub-Saha-

ran Africa and South Asia, and a third in North Africa and the rest of Asia, are self-employed – mainly in the informal sector.[24]

Far fewer women are employed in industry: some 16–17 per cent in Asia and Latin America, and 6 per cent in Africa.[25] The proportion of women in industry increased slightly between 1950 and 1980 in developed and developing regions, but growth slowed from the 1970s. Differences between countries have been pronounced. In the newly industrialized economies (NIEs), the Philippines and parts of central America, the share of women in manufacturing employment is as high as 40 per cent, often because of the predominance of women in free trade zones (see Chapter 5). An increasing proportion of industrial production, however, takes place in the informal sector through subcontracting.

MORE DEVELOPED REGIONS The most remarkable change has been the growth in service employment for women (see below), paralleled by a decline for both men and women in the agricultural sector and, more significantly, in manufacturing. The proportion of women working in the service sector rose from 33 to 58 per cent between 1950 and 1980. Currently, women make up about half of all workers in the service sector, and one third of those are in industry. Fewer than 5 per cent of women work in the agricultural sector of most European countries and of the United States.[26]

Women in manufacturing are concentrated in a small range of traditional and relatively labour-intensive 'light' industries, in particular foods, garments and textiles and shoes, plus the newer micro-electronics assembly. This is also true in the modern sector of developing countries, and in eastern Europe. Where mechanization and new technology have been intro-

Table 2.2: FEMALE SHARE OF MAJOR SECTOR, DEVELOPING COUNTRIES, 1950–2000

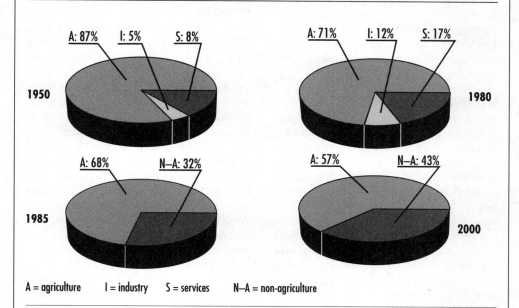

A = agriculture   I = industry   S = services   N–A = non-agriculture

SOURCE: ILO

Table 2.3: FEMALE SHARE OF MAJOR SECTORS, INDUSTRIALIZED COUNTRIES, 1950–2000

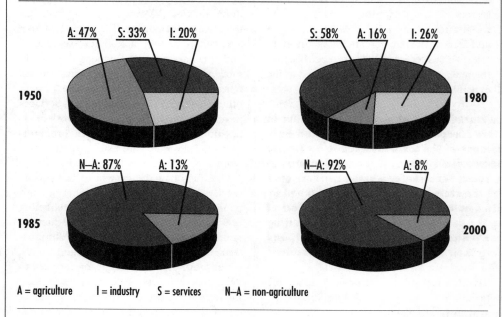

A = agriculture   I = industry   S = services   N–A = non-agriculture

SOURCE: ILO

23

duced, more or better-paid jobs have generally been created for men. Self-employment rates are much lower than in developing countries, an average of 15 per cent, but these reflect formal sector activity rather than informal.

ECONOMIES IN TRANSITION The political changes in central and eastern Europe and the former Soviet Union have had profound economic effects. Investment is slow, while political and economic uncertainty persists, and internal resources are stretched to the limit. The full employment policies of the socialist system have not survived the harsh realities of the market economy: the closure or rationalization of large state enterprises, cuts in government departments, the collapse of trade within the former Communist bloc, and falling internal demand are resulting in the loss of millions of jobs. Wages are also falling behind the spiralling rates of inflation.

In most countries more women than men are losing their jobs – in some because the sectors where they predominate are the worst affected, in many because child care and leave arrangements are being cut in an effort to reduce costs, and in most because the male workforce is being protected at the expense of the female.

From a market point of view, female labour in Eastern Europe is more expensive than male labour because of the costs involved in maternity and childcare provisions.... If the costs of providing the social benefits for women workers once borne by the state ... are now to be assumed by private employers, this will have the effect of reducing the demand for female labour, limiting women's access to full-time employment, and reducing their earnings in the formal sector.[27]

The political will to take positive action on behalf of women is also likely to diminish as women are playing a smaller role in the new parties and governments.

JOBS IN SERVICES: MADE FOR WOMEN? As noted above, much of the increase in women's employment has been in services. The growth of the service sector, whilst especially important in the developed regions, has global implications because a number of services are being rapidly internationalized, as manufacturing was in the 1970s. The service sector is already the main employer of women in all industrialized countries and the Latin American region, and of women in non-agricultural activity in other countries. Even in the informal sector, more women are in services than in production. Although it is difficult to measure, women appear to provide some two-thirds of services in the informal sector of selected African countries.[28]

Women work in a relatively narrow range of occupations at the lower levels of pay and responsibility: in health, education and social services; banking and insurance; hotel and catering; the retail trade; and personal services such as hairdressing and domestic work. Women typically make up the majority of sales staff, cleaners, kitchen assistants, nursing auxiliaries, secretaries and primary-school teachers.[29] Overall, more service jobs are part-time, casual, temporary or 'informal' than are jobs in other sectors. The new high-tech services have not brought new forms of work organization with them: computer programmers and designers are usually men, whilst women do the data entry.

One factor in the growth of the private service sector has been the number of companies that have expanded their marketing operations rather than direct production; another factor was the prosperity of industrialized countries in the 1960s and 1970s, which gave rise to a range of services to help people invest, save and spend their money. The public sector is a major employer in most countries, and an important employer of women in many. Women predominate in the public services of the Nordic countries, the United Kingdom and the United States, and average nearly 40 per cent of public sector workers in most other industrialized countries.[30] As a result of the setting of health and education targets, and government policies to ensure jobs for the qualified, the public services of many developing countries grew considerably from independence until the 1980s. The public sector often provided rare job opportunities for women: in a number of francophone African countries in the early 1980s, for example, it provided between two and five times the employment opportunities of the private sector.[32]

ISSUES IN WOMEN'S WORK The fact that women predominate in certain occupations, as well as at the lower levels of skill, responsibility and pay, is what is generally meant by job segregation. A recent publication from the ILO points out that the idea of 'concentration' should also be used, and indeed is often what we really mean when we talk about 'segregation'. The tendency for men and women to be employed in different occupations is segregation; the fact that women are overrepresented in a limited number of occupations or in lower grades is concentration.[33] What is important is the impact on women: their lack of opportunities in

WOMEN AS SERVANTS

Domestic service is almost a sector in itself. The numbers of women employed in it are vast. It is, for example, the major employer of women in much of Latin America. In three Latin American countries, domestic service accounted for nearly all the growth in women's employment in the informal sector between 1960 and 1980. In many parts of Asia and Africa young women – sometimes, but not necessarily, relatives – work as servants in households, large and small. The Anti-Slavery Society reports that some of these women are not so much servants as slaves, working without contracts and sometimes without pay – because of a clan or tribal connection, or a debt bondage, or because the young women's parents were paid for letting them go. The women can be very young, in fact children. Girls between the ages of six and fourteen are preferred in Bangladesh, for example, because women cost more and might attract the men. At puberty they are often simply sent away, to end up destitute or in prostitution.

'Siriah Mdlalose came to Johannesburg almost twenty years ago – and she will not be returning home to Vryheid for a very long time. On her wage as a domestic worker, she cannot afford frequent trips to visit her loved ones in the dusty Natal township of Bhakuzulu – a round trip of 1,400 miles.

'Siriah's day starts when she gets out of her bed raised on old paint cans above the concrete floor in the servant's quarters of the Wendywood mansion. She wakes the "Madam" and "Boss" with tea in bed, before making breakfast and preparing the children for school. She stays on her feet until about 9.00 pm when she flops exhausted on to her bed after washing the dinner dishes. She has to prepare her own food on a primus stove she bought herself, cooking one dish at a time. After sending money to her mother in Vryheid, she is left with very little to buy even the barest essentials. She is given Thursday off and works half a day on Sunday. But then what can she do when she does not have the means or the money to visit friends in the neighbouring suburbs?'[31]

PHOTO: ILO/J. MAILLARD

The high numbers of women in services

both formal and informal employment increases competition between them and keeps wages low.

HORIZONTAL SEGREGATION Horizontal segregation – or concentration – is about the clustering of women in certain occupations and in a limited number of activities within them. As noted above, particularly high numbers of women work in services, especially the personal and caring services. Women's participation in the industrial sector is generally lower than men's, and concentrated in a relatively narrow range of labour-intensive light industries. Where men and women work in the same industry, even the same factory, there are clear job boundaries, with women on the assembly line and men repairing machines and supervising, for example. A similar demarcation exists in the agricultural sector, sometimes assigning men to cash crops and women to subsistence farming, but also establishing a division of tasks within each.

Non-traditional occupations Various training and employment programmes have sought to promote the entry of women into occupations traditionally dominated by men, but these have not always been successful. Levels of performance by the women have generally equalled or exceeded those of men, but their isolation from other women, and sometimes overt harassment by male colleagues, has caused a high drop-out rate. An analysis of certain pilot schemes in the mid- and late 1980s led the ILO to conclude that improved training and labour planning, plus better links between the two, could bring about positive changes.[34] Training to equip women to take advantages of the job opportunities offered by new technology is seen as particularly important. More wide-ranging measures to change the values assigned to different occupations are also believed to have potential for bringing about change. These can be reinforced by action within the industries concerned. Some male-dominated sectors have taken initiatives to desegregate occupations. The International Maritime Organization, with assistance from the United Nations

Industrial Development Organization (UNIDO), has recently produced a plan of action for the integration of women in the maritime sector, covering women both at sea and in shore-based occupations.

The situation is continuing to evolve. Women in industrialized countries have made progress in professional occupations: as engineers, lawyers, doctors, and middle managers in industry. An OECD study found that the general trend was for segregation to diminish in all countries, although unevenly and rather slowly.[36] Outside the OECD, women have broken into the professions and non-traditional occupations in smaller numbers, but those concerned have often had a powerful impact as role models. The increasing number of girls in secondary schooling, and beyond, is also a hopeful indicator of change.

VERTICAL SEGREGATION Even where an occupation is to some extent mixed, women are usually in the less responsible, less secure and less well-paid jobs; where an occupation is predominantly female, men are still often found in the management positions: the head of a primary school, for example, or the shop manager. Worldwide, the proportion of women in managerial and decision-making positions is low; nowhere does it reflect the numbers of women in the labour force, and the higher you go up the job hierarchy, the fewer the women. Women make up less

STEPPING INTO THE UNKNOWN

More and more individual women have found the courage to step into the unknown, and by doing so make it a little bit easier for other women to follow in their footsteps. A good example is Sisi Beauty Charakupa, the first Zimbabwean woman to drive a taxi. She started driving taxis in 1984. She is married with two teenage children.

– *Why did you choose to become a taxi driver?*

'Workers' Day has always been most interesting to me, and I have always attended this annual event. In 1984 almost all the companies which displayed at this occasion had both male and female workers. I could not understand why companies like RIXI Taxis had no female workers. I decided to go to RIXI and look for a job. Not that my husband was pleased with this idea. But I managed to convince him,' she said.

– *How did your future employers react when you applied for the job?*

'It was not easy talking to those men. At first they thought I was joking. It took me two days to convince them that I was capable of being a taxi driver. I went on a road test and I had to drive one of the break-down cars. I passed the test but that was not the end. I learnt how to change a punctured tyre, I made my own cut-off switches. These are just a few of the things which men feel women should not do. But all this is not as hard as we are made to believe,' she said.

– *Would you recommend this job to other women?*

'The problem with most of us women is that we tend to think certain jobs are meant for men only. So far I have only heard of three women driving taxis. Please my sisters, do not be fooled by men. If you feel you want to do a certain job, do not stop and say, "What will men think?" Of course the men will try as much as they can to make you feel uncomfortable. This is when you learn to fight for yourself, and make them realise that you are also a human being. I would like to see more women driving taxis,' she said.[35]

than 5 per cent of the world's heads of state, heads of major corporations and top executives in international organizations; of the top 1,000 corporations in the United States, two are headed by women. Women represent, on average, under 10 per cent of members of parliament and 20 per cent of middle-level managers.[37]

Career paths and glass ceilings Quite substantial numbers of women find themselves on a level with male colleagues at an early stage in their careers, but ten years later the chances are that most of those men will be in more senior positions than the women – regardless of initial qualification, ability, or experience. At some point around the middle of most career ladders, there appears to be a 'glass ceiling' which prevents all but a few women from getting to the top. Why are women

---

WOMEN ON TOP?

The Journal of General Management sets out the main reasons that have been identified by various studies for women's underrepresentation in senior positions:

'1. Women themselves: lack of education and training; lack of a continuous career as a result of breaks for child-rearing and some preference for part-time working ...; and lack of the confidence or drive to succeed.

'2. Personnel policies and organisational career structures which ... are shaped by the traditions of a male career: lack of provision for career breaks and re-entry; lack of appropriate provision for women's management development; and lack of provision for flexible contracts at higher levels.

'3. Organisational climate and the attitudes of senior management: lack of awareness of the pervasiveness of masculine assumptions; lack of interest in the need for strategic change to increase the utilisation of female resources; and lack of support for the few women who do succeed.'[38]

---

underrepresented in management? While this may be seen as a symptom of women's subordination, specific mechanisms cause the concentration of women at the lower levels of responsibility, as listed in the box here.

In addition, many women are in jobs that have no prospects for advancement.

Pinpointing barriers helps to focus strategies for change. Training is obviously one key element, and is considered more fully in Chapter 6. Building gender-aware career paths or schemes into organizations, reviewing promotion processes, and monitoring the position of women are other positive measures which have been taken. Addressing the particular needs of workers with family responsibilities has been found to have a significant effect in keeping women within an organization and thus enhancing their chances of promotion. It is clear that once there is a commitment by management, plenty of ways are found to bring more women into responsible positions. How then are women to get this commitment from the top bosses and decision-makers? It is not in fact an unrealistic aim, given changing attitudes to women's employment, shortages of skilled labour, and a better understanding of what women have to offer. Changes in production organization, technology, and management practice, among other areas, require new and changing skills, as well as flexibility in the workforce. It is clearly not in the interests of corporate or state employers to deprive themselves of the potential offered by professional women.

The numbers of women in management increased in thirty-nine out of forty-one countries between 1985 and 1990;[39] in the United States their numbers doubled in the course of the 1980s. While most are still in middle management, the pressure on the higher positions is building up. It has also been pointed out that most of the men in

PHOTO: ILO/J. MAILLARD

Initiatives to de-segregate occupations: metal workers in Venezuela

top management today went to business school at a time when very few women did. Numbers of women who are trained and in training are now much higher, but time is needed for them to work their way up the system.

THE PAY GAP The difference in pay for men and women – be it in cash or kind, and including allowances, 'perks' and even food for work – is one of the clearest signs of inequality at the workplace. The widespread view of women as secondary earners and unskilled workers, as well as their lack of bargaining power, enables this discrimination to continue. In spite of equal pay legislation in most countries, the occupational segregation of men and women makes it very easy to apply different remuneration rates to 'men's work' and 'women's work'. As most women work outside the formal sector in any case, there are few

mechanisms available to strengthen their position.

In every country for which data exist, women's wage rates are lower than men's. In a few countries – including Iceland, France and Australia – the range is between 75 and 92 per cent of men's wages; more report between 55 and 75 per cent. In some countries women's wages are about half, or just over, the rate for men – including the Republic of Korea, Japan and Brazil. The average gap is between 30 and 40 per cent.[40] Women predominate in jobs that are poorly paid and lack a career structure, and at the lower levels of responsibility in jobs where the workforce is mixed. Other factors that contribute to the pay gap include the more limited opportunities for women to do overtime, night and shift work where substantial premiums may be paid; the interruption to the accumulation of seniority because of child-bearing; and the greater numbers of women on part-time, temporary and casual contracts. All types of disadvantage are reinforced – or have been until recently – by the fact that male-dominated trade unions have either deliberately negotiated agreements to men's advantage, or have failed to take active measures on behalf of the most poorly paid and precarious workers.

SOCIAL SECURITY Two sorts of bias are inherent in many social protection schemes: in their origins, at least, they were geared to the needs and structures of the Western industrialized workforce, and they were geared also to the earnings pattern and record of the male breadwinner. Most social security schemes have now addressed the issue of direct sexual discrimination and no longer assume that women are dependants, but this has not solved the problem of income security faced by women of all ages, especially older women. In the United States, for example, 25 per cent of women aged over sixty-five live in poverty, compared with only 9 per cent of men in the same age group.[41] So long as social security provisions relate to earnings records of workers, women will remain at a disadvantage: in general they have shorter and more interrupted work histories, and a lower level of earnings; and benefits are often poorer for those in junior, part-time and temporary positions where women are overrepresented. These points can apply to private as well as statutory schemes. As a result, although women should accumulate entitlements in their own rights, adequate compensation must be built into schemes in recognition of women's different work histories. A universal pension, and an element that is means-tested rather than earnings-related, would also help to ensure that older women do not fall through the social net.[42]

In developing countries, social security rarely covers more than 10 per cent of the population, and it is concentrated in the formal sector and main urban centres. The most commonly provided programme is old age, invalidity, and death insurance; the least common are unemployment insurance and family allowances.[43] Few women are included, because of their predominance in informal and agricultural work. The lack of public resources and the poorer institutional development in many developing countries mean that a combination of public, private and voluntary measures will be required in order to make coverage more widely available, as well as smaller-scale, less formal systems. Even if governments are not able to provide all the funding, however, the responsibility for the organization of social protection remains theirs.

FAMILY RESPONSIBILITIES No discussion of what women do would be complete without referring to the question of domestic responsibilities, and women's 'double burden'. Whether or not women are in paid employment, whether or not they are working in farms, other family enterprises or their own businesses, they are still responsible for the management of the home. The entry of women onto the labour market has not yet had the effect of relieving them of a share of housework and child care – either through an increase in public or company provision, or through men taking more responsibility. Women simply work longer hours in order to fit all their work in. This phenomenon is called the 'double shift' or 'double burden' – for obvious reasons.

Even though children are tomorrow's workers and citizens, they are seen today as the private and personal responsibility of their families. The fact that child care has been made widely available under certain circumstances shows that its provision is primarily a matter of employment policy and political will – or lack of it. During the Second World War, for example, facilities became available as increasing numbers of women were needed to work in factories and essential services. After the war, not only did most of these facilities close down but new theories suddenly emerged which threatened dire consequences if young children did not stay in close contact with their mothers.

A similar trend may be observed now in most of the countries of the former Communist bloc in Europe. Crèches and nurseries were very widely available under the previous system and the great majority of women were in the labour force. Such are the economic strains of the transition to a free market economy, however, that fewer employers are providing facilities. The unwritten agenda is the need to 'encourage' women back into the home as one way of coping with spiralling unemployment.

The changing composition of families puts an extra burden on many women but may also lead to changes in social organization and attitudes. It will take some time for stereotypes of the family – which have a number of common features across different societies – to be replaced by something

Table 2.4: HOURS WORKED PER WEEK BY WOMEN AND MEN

TOTAL WORKING TIME INCLUDING UNPAID HOUSEWORK (HOURS PER WEEK)

SOURCE: THE WORLD'S WOMEN (based on studies conducted between 1976 and 1988)

closer to reality. When this happens, perhaps the idea of the male breadwinner will go with it. Such issues will, it is hoped, be central to the discussion in the course of 1994 – the Year of the Family (see *Women and the Family* in this series). Although the gendered construction of family life gives men more control and freedom of movement, they are losers as well. They lose time with their families, the chance to develop emotional and caring qualities, and the sharing of the wage-earning burden. 'I feel a bit trapped by work, I suppose. I'd love to spend more time with the kids so that I felt closer to them' (Mike, member of the British Transport and General Workers' Union).[46] Transforming the sexual division of labour must mean a redistribution of power but it also offers the possibility of a more rounded and fulfilling role for men as well as women.

WORKING TODAY: FLEXIBLE OR PRECARIOUS? ☐ Labour market

flexibility is defined as 'changes in the regulations, contracts, customs and practices that govern the labour market so as to make it easier to hire, and more especially fire, workers'.[47] Employers argue that they require freedom of manoeuvre in order to respond flexibly to demand, and to increase profitability. The drive towards flexibility has contributed to a steady rise in non-standard forms of employment such as part-time working and contracting out. At least half of all the employment created in France, Germany, the Netherlands, Luxembourg and Spain in the 1980s was for workers on temporary contracts. Many non-standard jobs are held by women, and it should be recognized that such jobs have provided a way for women to enter the labour market.

Flexibility need not necessarily be to the disadvantage of the employee, and the very concept 'non-standard' raises the question of what the standard or norm should be.

CONTRASTING VIEWS OF HOUSEWORK

'You all know that even when women have full rights, they still remain factually downtrodden because all housework is left to them. In most cases housework is the most unproductive, the most barbarous and the most arduous work a women can do. It is exceptionally petty and does not include anything that would in any way promote the development of the woman.'

V.I. Lenin, revolutionary leader[44]

On the other hand ...
'What is demeaning about looking after the home I live in? One of the greatest pleasures in life is to sleep between nice, crisp sheets. What is bad in preparing them for myself? But in the West you learn that such jobs are low. And of course, the makers of society give such jobs to women. So what is the result? The most important chores that make us human are regarded as low.... In our kitchens [children] learn ...and we send them out from our kitchens to be grown men and women. What greater work is there than that? I do not think it low. Those who wish to control and influence the future generations by giving birth and nurturing the young should not be looked down upon. If I had my way it would be the highest-paid job in the world. We think it is low because society says so. But it is time we said, "It is not so. We will train all people – men and women – in housework" '.

Buchi Emecheta, Nigerian writer[45]

There is a danger of judging ... the operation of the labour market according to standards which see full-time ... life-long jobs, based on carefully demarcated craft skills, as the desirable 'norm' to which all workers ... aspire.... This is a male norm that most women have never enjoyed, and many women do not want.[48]

Women's groups in the 1960s and 1970s were already arguing that greater flexibility in working hours would benefit workers and their families, and some experiments in 'flexitime' date from then. Trade unions in industrialized countries now routinely bargain for a range of leave and break arrangements, as well as for reductions in total working hours. Increased costs and losses in productivity are not inevitable: a better sharing out of hours of work is likely to increase motivation and productivity, and new technology can also play an important part.

This does not, however, solve the problem of the precarious element in non-standard working, the lack of security for workers with 'casual' contracts, and their poor pay and conditions. A related problem is the erosion of the organizational base of the workforce and the increased decentralization of collective bargaining. Diane Elson argues that the issue of workers' rights should be addressed as such, rather than the whole notion of flexibility opposed. As long as the rights of workers are safeguarded, the disintegration of traditional forms of 'regular work' may create the basis for progressive social transformations. The challenge for the social partners is to improve the terms of flexibility, bring equal opportunities to standard and non-standard employment, and ease movement between flexible arrangements and the mainstream. Trade unions are coming late to these ideas, though Sweden has provided a model for some time. The unions

there have worked in collaboration with the government to introduce legislation in this area: the Parliamentary Bill on Equal Opportunities for the 1990s states that one of the main social challenges is to recast the terms prevailing in working life – job organization, forms of work, and working hours – in order to create a more balanced situation between women and men, and between home and work.

CONCLUSION ☐ The issues in women's work are shaped by the structural disparities of the gender system. Women do not enter the labour market – be it formal or informal – on the same basis as men, nor do they operate within it on equal terms. The social and economic roles allotted to men and women limit women's access to the means of production – from credit to training opportunities – and result in the crowding of women into a limited number of occupations and markets. The lower wages and prices they command, and the pressure on their time from their unpaid domestic activities, mean that women everywhere are working longer hours than men for considerably less income, and with less control over the decision-making processes that affect their lives and work.

But the situation is not static, and the full impact of women's increasing participation in waged labour and own-account activities has yet to be seen. What is especially significant is the degree of change that has taken place in just a generation. Although the percentage of women is low in the modern industrial sector of most developing countries, and in senior and managerial positions generally, it has increased. The significance of this increase has been out of all proportion to the numbers, because it has shown that change is possible. Social and economic roles, occupational stereotypes, women's capabilities – indeed, the basic division of labour – once seemed carved in stone but are now shown to be susceptible to reshaping. Recognition is growing of women's multiple roles and the value not only of their productive but also of their reproductive contribution. Traditional work norms are being questioned, new forms of labour organization are being developed, and the relationship between work and leisure is being recast.

This has far-ranging implications for social and economic planning, including employment policy, social insurance programmes, and development planning. We are moving towards a new way of looking at work, which could in turn help us to develop more imaginative and comprehensive ways of tackling fundamental issues such as unemployment and the lack of social protection. We should view as work all human activity that is of value to society, but recognize that it does not all lead directly to the creation or distribution of income. If the concept of work is separated from that of employment, and the creation of wealth is separated from its distribution, it might be possible to work out more equitable ways of providing a living, social wage for all people.[49]

1. Quoted in Wendy Edmond and Suzie Fleming (eds), *All Work and No Pay: Women, Housework and the Wages Due*, Falling Wall Press, London, 1975.
2. Guy Standing, 'Labour force participation and development', quoted in Shirley Nuss, *Women in the World of Work: Statistical Analysis and Projections to the year 2000*, ILO, Geneva, 1989, p. 16.
3. Nuss.
4. United Nations, *The World's Women: Trends and Statistics, 1970–1990*, United Nations, New York, 1991.
5. Ibid.
6. Ibid., p. 83.
7. ILO, *World Labour Report*, No. 6, 1993.
8. ILO, *World Labour Report*, No. 5, 1992, p. 22.
9. United Nations Food and Agricultural Organization (FAO), *Gender Issues in Rural Food Security in Developing Countries*, FAO, Rome, 1990.
10. Aili Mari Tripp, 'The impact of crisis and economic reform on women in urban Tanzania', in Lourdes Beneria and Shelley Feldman (eds), *Unequal Burden: Economic Crises, Persistent Poverty and Women's Work*, Westview Press, Boulder and Oxford, 1992.
11. 'How the other half moves', *POPULI*, July–August 1993.
12. *The World's Women*.
13. ILO, *World Labour Report*, No. 5, 1992.
14. 'How the other half moves'.
15. Ibid.
16. Luís Fina Sanglas, 'The outlook on the European labour market', in European Trade Union Institute, *The Future of Work*, ETUI, Brussels, 1990, p. 19.
17. Nuss, p. 36.
18. 'Demographic transition and ageing', in Tarek M. Shuman *et al.* (eds), *Population Aging: International Perspectives*, United Nations Population Division, New York, forthcoming.
19. 'Ageing women and their contribution to development', *Women 2000*, No. 3, 1991.
20. International Confederation of Free Trade Unions (ICFTU), *Equality: The Continuing Challenge – Strategies for Success*, ICFTU, Brussels, 1991.
21. ILO, *Part-time Work*, report to the Eightieth Session of the International Labour Conference, 1993.
22. Ibid.
23. Nuss.
24. *The World's Women*.
25. Ibid.
26. Nuss.
27. Valentine Moghadam, *Privatization and Democratization in Central and Eastern Europe: the Gender Dimension*, United Nations University World Institute for Development Economics Research (UNU/WIDER), Helsinki, 1992, p. 19.
28. *The World's Women*.
29. ICFTU.
30. Public Services International, *Paths to Power*, background paper for Second World Women's Conference, PSI, Ferney-Voltaire, 1992.
31. Reproduced from the *South African Sunday Star*, 27 August 1989, in Scottish Education and Action for Development, *Shoulder to Shoulder: a Teaching Pack on Women Organizing*.
32. ILO, *Women at Work*, No. 1, 1984.
33. Janet Siltanen, Jennifer Jarman and Robert M. Blackburn, *Gender Inequality in the Labour Market: Occupational Concentration and Segregation, a Manual on Methodology*, ILO, Geneva, 1992.
34. ILO, *Women at Work*, No. 2, 1986.
35. 'Women's achievements', in *Speak Out/Taurai/Khulumani*, No. 17, 1991.
36. Organisation for Economic Cooperation and Development, *The Integration of Women into the Economy*, OECD, Paris, 1985.
37. *The World's Women*.
38. Sheila Rothwell, 'Manpower matters: women's career developments', in *Journal of General Management*, No. 4, Vol. 11, 1986.
39. 'Unequal race to the top', in ILO, *World of Work*, No. 2, 1993.
40. ILO, *General Survey of the Committee of Experts on Equal Remuneration*, ILO, Geneva, 1986.
41. 'Ageing women and ... development'.
42. Report of the Director General to the Eightieth Session of the International Labour Conference, ILO, Geneva, 1993.
43. Valentine Moghadam and N. Folbre, 'Equality and social security', draft report to the ILO Tripartite Meeting, Geneva, 1993.
44. V.I. Lenin, *Collected Works*, Vol. XXX, Progress Publishers, Moscow.
45. Quoted in *New Internationalist*, No. 149, 1985.
46. Quoted in Trades Union Congress, *Working Women: a TUC Handbook for all Trade Unionists*, TUC, London, 1991.

47. Diane Elson, 'Appraising recent developments in the world market for nimble fingers: accumulation, regulation, organisation', paper presented to an international workshop on Women Organizing in the Process of Industrialization, held at the Institute of Social Studies, The Hague, 1991.

48. Ibid., pp. 9–10.

49. Gabriel Fragnière, 'The changing value of work', in European Trade Union Institute, *The Future of Work*, ETUI, Brussels, 1990.

3 RURAL EMPLOYMENT

Don't bother talking to the women. What do they know?

INDIAN VILLAGER TO SURVEY TEAM[1]

Agricultural productivity cannot be ... increased, nor can rural poverty be alleviated, unless women's access to key ... resources and services is substantially improved. The consequences of patriarchy ... are very expensive – **FAO[2]**

THREE-QUARTERS OF WOMEN all over the world live in rural areas and most of them work in agriculture and a wide range of related activities. Women grow rice, cereals and vegetables; pick fruit and tea; tend goats and chickens; smoke fish; weave and spin; make pots, beer, clothes; market and trade – to list only a few.[3]

TRENDS IN RURAL EMPLOYMENT □

New consideration is being given to the rural sector and agricultural development, as a response to the limited employment possibilities in the formal sector and the increased pressure on the urban informal sector. Whilst agriculture has been and remains the backbone of the economies of most developing countries, during the 1960s and 1970s it was viewed primarily as a resource for the urban–industrial sector, which was the main target of development policy. The relative neglect of the rural economy may also be seen in the lack of available statistics, though the nature of rural employment is an added difficulty. Most rural workers are self-employed or unpaid workers on family farms or enterprises; where there is wage employment it is predominantly casual, temporary or seasonal.

It is estimated that some 70 per cent of people in developing countries live in rural areas and that 60 per cent depend mainly on agriculture for their livelihood. In all the developing regions except Latin America a higher proportion of the female labour force works in agriculture than of the male. The share of agriculture in total employment has been gradually declining over a number of years; it fell from 71 to 63 per cent between 1970 and 1985 – and further in the newly industrialized economies (NIEs) and other rapidly industrializing countries.

This decline is associated with the enormous movement of people from rural to urban areas and with the spread of small to medium-sized 'rural towns'. Between 1970 and 1985 the urban population grew two to three times faster than the rural population in all developing regions. In Latin America there was virtually no growth at all in the rural areas: the cities absorbed the increased population, and urban unemployment and the informal sector both grew throughout the 1980s. Although the formal sector weakened in Africa over the same period, with little job creation and declining incomes, urbanization continued unabated. There is starting to be evidence of movement back to villages in some countries because of pressure on the urban informal sector, and more favourable prices for certain agricultural products.

WAGE LABOUR AND NON-FARM ACTIVITIES □

Whilst most rural workers are in agriculture, others may work in rural industries and construction, artisanal production, community services or trade. The divisions between occupations are seldom clear, and women in particular undertake multiple activities at the same time and at different points in the year. High numbers of people in each region are self-employed, especially in sub-Saharan Africa, where access to land is

Planting rice in Bangladesh: women make up an important part of the rural labour force in all regions

37

Table 3.1: THE PACE OF URBANIZATION

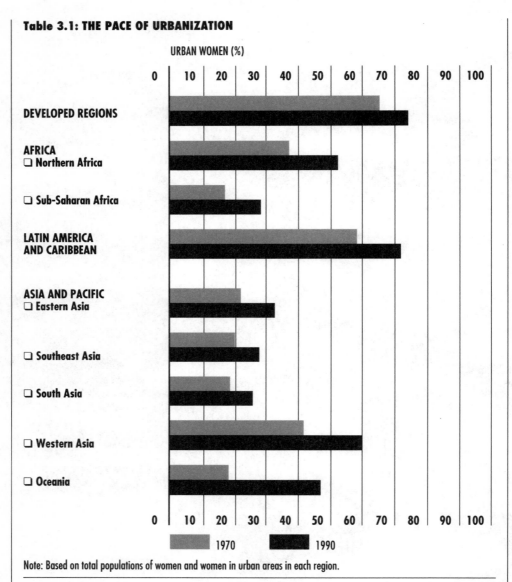

URBAN WOMEN (%)

Note: Based on total populations of women and women in urban areas in each region.

SOURCE: THE WORLD'S WOMEN

more widespread than elsewhere. In this region women tend to be unpaid labourers on their husbands' or household land, and to cultivate in their own right – often both at the same time.

Rural wage labour is more common in Latin America, much of Asia, and North Africa. Land holdings are more concentrated, and landlessness and near-landlessness are widespread. In Bangladesh, landlessness has tripled since independence. In several Asian countries wage-earning has become an important part of agricultural employment, but much of it is on a casual basis. Women's waged employment is increasing in all these regions, though their wages remain extremely low, often half those of men's. In Latin America, the rural and urban work-forces are more integrated than elsewhere and agriculture takes a number of its workers from the towns. Much temporary migration takes place as both men and women move from one big estate to the next as work becomes available, with and without their families. Women are used for some of the most labour-intensive tasks in the production of cash crops, such as coffee picking.

In all regions, women make up an important part of the labour force on plantations. Sometimes they are hired in their own right, sometimes as part of a family work team. In almost all cases their wages are lower than men's, although their work is heavy, tiring and often dangerous, as plantations make intensive use of chemicals. Living conditions are often of very poor standard, cramped and insanitary, and with rarely even basic amenities for recreation or the care and schooling of children. Staff at the International Federation of Plantation, Agriculture and Allied Workers (IFPAAW) say that the conditions of employment on many estates are little better than serfdom.

Non-farm activities range from trading and handicrafts to industries such as spinning and milling. They are becoming increasingly important as neither formal sector nor agriculture is able to provide jobs for the rapidly growing labour force, more and more of whom are without land. In Asian countries between 20 and 40 per cent of the rural labour force is engaged in non-agricultural activities. A lower proportion has been reported in other regions, but data collection is particularly difficult and local studies suggest much higher figures. It seems clear that women's participation in these activities is generally increasing,

especially among landless women. Non-farm activities may also supplement an income from agriculture; women fit them in as they can around both agricultural and domestic tasks.

GROWING HUNGER ☐ Per capita food production in Africa has slowly declined since the 1960s; between 1970 and 1982, while the population grew by nearly 3 per cent a year, the increase in food production was 0.7 per cent for the whole period.[4] The figures for individual countries are dramatic. Zaïre, for example, a net exporter of food in the 1960s, was spending some $300 million a year on food imports by the 1980s.[5] In 1993, the development charity Oxfam reported that severe malnourishment was affecting 300 million people in Africa.

The reasons are complex. Recurrent droughts, the destruction of forests, inappropriate farming practices, and the pressure of increasing population have led to the degradation and desertification of large areas. At the same time, these problems have been compounded by policies that fail to protect vulnerable areas and to provide alternative grazing or arable land, that positively drive people to marginal, unstable areas, and that promote exports or cash cropping at the expense of food security. In Asia, landlessness is increasing among the poor and contributing to further poverty. Reinforcing all these problems has been the neglect of the role of women as food producers, resulting in a range of inappropriate policies and measures.

PRODUCING FOOD: THE WORK OF WOMEN ☐ Women directly produce about half the world's food, and they process and prepare almost all of it. For women everywhere, daily life is a juggling act as they try to fit in a range of tasks and responsibilities. In the rural areas this situation is at its most extreme: most women

Women process and prepare nearly all the world's food: grinding corn in Costa Rica

are directly involved in the production of food for family consumption, and often for sale or exchange as well; many hire out their labour if they can, and trade or make handicrafts; at the same time, there is a constant range of domestic tasks which have to be done, most of them related to the preparation of food and the care of children.

We work approximately 16 hours a day inside and outside the house. I work with the *cabuya* [the dried inner fibres of cactus] like a man, combing it, spinning it, and cutting it down. Then I can 'rest'. I do the things that need to be done in the house. That's what they call our 'rest'. We leave one job to do another.[6]

HOURS AND TASKS OF MEN AND WOMEN □ *The World's Women* reports average hours worked per week as between sixty and sixty-five in most of Asia and Latin America, and over 65 hours in Africa. It stresses that poor women work much harder than these averages – between sixty and ninety hours a week – and also that in many developing regions women's working hours have become longer, 'just [trying] to maintain their meagre living standards of a decade ago'.[7] Women also work longer hours than men. The widest gaps are in Africa and Asia, where women average twelve to thirteen more hours a week than men.

AFRICA Women make up over 70 per cent of the agricultural labour force in Africa. Men clear the land at the outset of a cultivation cycle, but otherwise women frequently do the planting, weeding, harvesting and processing of food crops with little or no male intervention. A study in Zambia found that the extent of a family's productivity depended largely on the number of females available for work.[8]

LACK OF OFFICIAL STATISTICS
Official statistics on the participation of women in food and agricultural production are still very scarce. This is a major obstacle to the incorporation of gender issues into food and agricultural policies, and an impediment in monitoring and evaluating rural development programmes. Planners tend to underestimate or ignore:

- the nature and scope of women's separate and autonomous operations;
- the extent of the reliance of men on women's labour and inputs;
- the uneven distribution of income and resources within the household.

Nevertheless, the interaction between men's and women's agricultural roles is complex: men may produce food crops different from those of women, rather than non-food crops only, and women produce crops for cash as well as for subsistence.[9] An essential element of women's farming in many African countries is its dual nature: women are engaged in independent farming as well as working on the fields of male household members. This latter work is usually unpaid, but sometimes payment in cash or kind is made between husbands and wives in return for their labour.

ASIA In East and Southeast Asia men's and women's tasks are distinct, but less possibility exists for women to exercise even limited control over certain crops or plots of land. In some countries, however, women manage to collect and gather quite substantial quantities of foods and raw materials from the forests and countryside. Among the most widespread of women's jobs are sowing, transplanting, weeding and processing, but men's contribution is more integrated and complementary, especially in rice production.[10] Many women work as waged labourers; increasing

Table 3.2: HOW THE WORK IS DIVIDED, AFRICA (% OF TOTAL LABOUR IN HOURS)

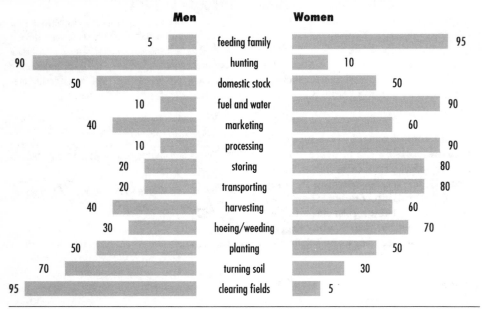

	Men		Women
feeding family	5		95
hunting	90		10
domestic stock	50		50
fuel and water	10		90
marketing	40		60
processing	10		90
storing	20		80
transporting	20		80
harvesting	40		60
hoeing/weeding	30		70
planting	50		50
turning soil	70		30
clearing fields	95		5

Source: Commonwealth Secretariat

numbers supplement their income by out-work for local manufacturers or agents.

In her study of the mechanization of rice production in west Malaysia, Cecilia Ng includes an interview with a farming couple. Napsiah and Mat have half an acre of land, all they could afford to buy. Renting is difficult because landowners want cash in advance, rather than after the harvest as they used to. Both Napsiah and Mat work on their plot but they cannot produce enough to feed the family. Mat, the husband, also works in a rice processing mill but does not earn enough to cover all their needs. Before mechanization, Napsiah used to get waged work when the rice was transplanted and harvested; now she looks after the children of the community teacher and helps a relative to make cakes. She cuts down expenses by hand weeding their rice plot, rather than using weed-killer, and she tends some mango trees and sells the fruit. Their oldest daughter has gone to the city to work in an electronics factory.[11]

LATIN AMERICA In other regions the female share in the agricultural labour force, at least in field work, is lower but there appears to have been severe underestimation. In Latin America, the culture of the male breadwinner is so strong that almost by definition only men's economic activities count as work. Women and men alike tend to categorize women's work, including sowing and harvesting, as housework because it is unpaid. Women in Guatemala, for example, reported that they were simply 'helping' their husbands when they raised and sold small animals.[12]

Figures that show Latin American women providing 10 to 20 per cent of agricultural labour are belied by accounts such as those contained in Audrey Bronstein's book *The Triple Struggle: Latin American Peasant Women*. Bronstein lived for some months in rural villages, observing the

women's work, talking and listening. It is clear from her account that during their waking hours the women work virtually non-stop, combining field work with other activities, such as spinning and weaving, inside and near the house. In Ecuador men often migrate to the towns or large estates looking for work, and women are in sole charge of the family plot and all the activities necessary to sustain the extended family. In El Salvador women support large families through intensive work on tiny smallholdings, supplemented by work on the large estates at harvest time, when all the family members go from one estate to another selling their labour. Permanent migration to the cities is very high. Bronstein also quotes a study conducted in Bolivia which found women not only engaged in all the activities of agricultural production, including marketing, but also spending more hours on all of them than did men.[13]

SECLUDED WOMEN A number of assumptions tend to be made about women's contribution to the agriculture of certain regions because of their lower participation in field work.

In the cultivation of rice in Bangladesh, for instance, men can be seen at work – preparing the fields, sowing and harvesting, and taking the finished product to market. But the many tasks performed by women, such as threshing, parboiling, husking, winnowing, sieving and storing the rice, go unseen – and therefore to a great extent disregarded.[14]

It has become clear from a number of studies that women in secluded societies participate in a wide range of farm and non-farm activities inside the house. A study of a Muslim village in northern Nigeria showed that seclusion did not stop women from engaging in trade and in processing food for sale. Children were used as go-between where this was necessary, for example in contacts with a supplier.[15]

There is not, however, a simple equation between Muslim societies and the seclusion of women, or even a low female participation in field work. While official statistics may put a low figure on women's agricultural activity, local studies show rates that are up to four times higher. The Central Agricultural Cooperative Union in Egypt has found that the range of women's agricultural tasks is steadily increasing due to a falling supply of rural labour – mainly the result of migration to the towns. Poverty can break down even strict social taboos, and women work outside the home when they, and the family, have no other choice. On the other hand, cultural barriers such as seclusion put a brake on the potential of women to expand their economic activities, for example by finding new markets.

COMMON EXPERIENCES, DIFFERENT LIVES Rural women are not, of course, a homogeneous group. The pressures on and the ambitions of a woman farmer in Ghana are quite different from those of the 'untouchable' landless labourer in India, and from those of the grandmother who heads the marketing committee of her village co-operative in China. Class is a determinant of power everywhere, and a hierarchy based on age remains important in many areas. In some countries caste and ethnic origin impact particularly severely on people's access to resources. Most rural women would find that their lives had points in common: they work longer hours than men, most of their work is unpaid, and their share of household income and decision making is not in proportion with

ILLUSTRATION: FAO/RAPA/KEES PUTMAN

Women work longer hours than men

their labour. This is why it is so important to recognize the different rights, responsibilities and assets of all the members of a household, and not to assume that income and expenditure are evenly shared.

ACCESS TO RESOURCES □ In order to grow and/or process food, women need a number of inputs, most basically land and labour; for those seeking to increase their productivity and incomes, other inputs are required, especially credit, improved technology, and training or extension services. Women have unequal access to, and control over, all these resources. An ILO workshop on women and land concluded that the processes of change in rural areas, especially population pressure and modern forms of land exploitation, were weakening women's access to the factors of production, including land, and resulting in declining food security at the household level.[16]

LAND Land provides not just the basis of production for the farm, smallholding or vegetable strip but the source of water, fuel, free foods and materials used in non-food production, such as clay for pots and dyes for cloth. Land titles also give access to other resources, most importantly credit, for which they serve as collateral. Many factors, from colonization to current land reform – and including cash cropping, mechanization, population growth and land erosion – have brought about profound changes in land use and land management. Even in Africa, where land ownership rates are highest, the availability of reasonable-quality land is becoming low in relation to the population.

Women's land rights are limited in all regions: their rights are generally derived from their husbands or other men (usually family members, sometimes village chiefs), and are thus conditional and insecure. Where men and women work separate plots, as in many African countries, women have the use of their land but not necessarily ownership, and their rights might not survive the death of a spouse. Laws defining women's status, and those governing marriage, property and inheritance, may all be incompatible with the principle of equal rights for women. Even where ownership and inheritance laws have been reformed, women do not necessarily have more secure rights in practice. Local custom and women's own lack of information are barriers to change.

Women in Tamil Nadu, India, complained that as the land they worked was not in their names, they would lose their incomes as well as their homes in the event of the death of their husbands, or divorce. With the support of the Community Services Guild, a local NGO [non-governmental organization], the women put pressure on the district collector to create joint *pattas* **(ownership titles). Nineteen men had agreed to this and after a year of petitions to the authorities, 19 joint** *pattas* **were made. The next year more than 100 were made, and a legal procedure has now been set up for the purpose.[17]**

Land reform and settlement Women's access to land is determined not only within the household and community but also by their household's place in society. Overall there is an increasing concentration of land in the hands of the wealthy – both individuals and companies. Land reform schemes, however, have rarely worked to women's benefit. As the FAO observes:

'In general, women have not been subjects of the agrarian reforms ... however in no case has the impact of reform been gender neutral.'[18]

Land reform schemes may replace a complex system of land use and tenure where women have certain rights in common law and local practice if not in legislation. The new land titles are almost invariably assigned to male heads of household, regardless of women's economic contribution to the household, their customary rights, or the increasing number of households headed by a woman. The services provided are also directed to the men: this was the conclusion of a review of settlement schemes in Indonesia, Malaysia, Sri Lanka and Papua New Guinea.[19]

In Tanzania, all rights were given to men when village land was allocated; no provision was made in law for widows, separated or divorced women. In contrast to traditional practice, men were able to sell or rent land without their wives' permission. In Kenya and Burkina Faso, among other schemes, the amount of land allocated to the household plot was smaller than women's traditional food fields, which had allowed them to sell small surpluses.[20] In Sri Lanka, women lost the right to own land after the death of their husbands – a particularly

severe reversal in a country where inheritance rights were traditionally shared by brothers and sisters.[21]

Experiments with land settlement suggest that benefits are obtained when rights to or ownership of land pass to a group of women. Not only does this enable them to pool their labour and other resources but it protects them against male appropriation and control.[22]

ENERGY AND WATER The land is not only used for cultivation. Two of women's central responsibilities are the gathering of fuelwood from fallow and common land and the fetching of water. The degradation of forests, wastelands and grazing areas, coupled with the privatization and commercialization of land, is resulting in a rural energy crisis. This affects women disproportionately and in a number of ways: in countries as far apart as Indonesia, Mozambique and Peru women are working longer hours to collect fuel and water, and are finding it more and more difficult to get what they need.

Women adopt a number of strategies to deal with this; an increasingly common one is to prepare food less often. In some parts of West Africa and many areas of the Andes, cooked meals have been reduced to one every other day, resulting in a drop in the level of nutrition. Another solution has been to replace fuelwood supplies with agricultural residues ... [thus depriving] the soil of their fertilizing effect and of humus.[23]

Fuel is necessary not only for cooking but also for other income-raising activities, such as fish smoking, beer brewing and brick making. Forests are also a source of fodder and raw materials. It has been proved that the collection of fuelwood is not a major cause of deforestation. The main causes are large-scale lumbering, the expansion of agriculture and grazing, and

urban growth. Women need to be involved in the development of policies that on the one hand improve management and conservation, and on the other increase women's rights to trees and their use. A positive trend is one away from reforestation based on a purely commercial concept of forestry – which restricts the access of poor people to the forests – towards social or community forestry. The FAO found that although early schemes failed to take into account their differential impact on men and women, more recent programmes have emphasized gender roles and needs.[24]

An interesting area of technical co-operation has been support for wasteland development in India through women's organizations. In 1981 a group of sixty-four tribal women in west Bengal formed an organization to promote land-based employment as an alternative to seasonal migrant labour. Land degradation and population growth had diminished local employment opportunities, and contractors were exploiting women's weak bargaining power and illiteracy. Working as a group, the women began to improve the returns from their existing activities and to start new ones. In 1982 they secured collective ownership of 9 acres of donated wasteland. Since then, some 350,000 woman days of paid labour have been generated, 300 acres have been reforested, and an additional 500 acres have been offered to the organization for development.[25]

Droughts and falling water tables are also forcing women to spend more time fetching water, or to divert cash resources to buy it if they can. Fetching water is one of women's most time-consuming tasks: women and girls in selected African countries were found to spend between five and seventeen hours a week getting water, and in three

Asian countries between four and seven hours.[26] While piping water to villages is one solution, it is clearly not a universal priority for politicians and, where it occurs, women do not necessarily benefit fully. They are rarely consulted over the siting of pipes or given secure rights to their use. Where women participate in, or control, investment in water supplies it can make an enormous difference to the quality of their lives, as well as to their productivity. Mexican women taking part in a UNIFEM project decided to use a loan fund to buy a community water pump. The pump made such a difference to their lives that they started a project to make and distribute the pumps at a factory built by their association.[27]

CREDIT The availability of credit is essential for improving productivity and enhancing income, and also, at times, for making up seasonal shortfalls. Short-term credit may be for seeds and fertilizers, longer-term credit for tools or animals, and perhaps to set up a small-scale enterprise, such as a poultry farm. In most developing countries, small farmers have limited access to credit, and women farmers especially. An analysis of credit schemes in five African countries where women predominate in food production found that women received less than 10 per cent of the credit directed to smallholders, and just 1 per cent of the total credit directed to agriculture.[28]

This is the result in part of their lack of collateral (land title or livestock) required to guarantee loans, and in part of their exclusion from male-oriented information networks and extension services. Women's potential productivity and ability to repay loans are also frequently underestimated, or even ridiculed, although their participation in the schemes to which they have been admitted shows a good record of repayment, and yields as good as or better than men's.[29] Denied access to private or public credit from outside, women have often taken measures to help themselves, ranging from traditional group savings schemes to associations and co-operatives with a range of economic and social objectives.

MARKETS Neither land nor credit can ensure that you are able to sell what you produce, let alone get a fair price for it. Factors that can limit women's access to markets, and their possibilities of expanding their markets, include: control by male family members over markets or marketing decisions; the operations of agents and middlemen; limits on women's mobility; and lack of information, management skills and contacts. Some of these can be overcome by joint marketing: very successful associations and co-operatives have been formed, especially when – perhaps with outside assistance – women have been able to tackle a range of barriers in a comprehensive way (see Chapter 8).

According to circumstances, some groups have placed more emphasis on increasing women's bargaining power so that they can bypass middlemen and interact with markets from a position of strength. Others have focused on market expansion: a grouping of organizations of poor women producers in Gujarat decided to break into the large market of government departments and publicly funded institutions. They lobbied the state government and convinced the Chief Minister to give them first preference without tender, in view of their unequal opportunities on the open market. A government resolution was subsequently passed to this effect.[30] Under the Export Production Villages scheme in Sri Lanka, the processing of agricultural produce is organized on a co-operative basis at the village level. The mainly female rural producers are then linked with export markets through larger local firms.[31] An

important element of the scheme is the diversification of both products and markets, in response to the fact that women tend to produce similar products for limited markets – thus increasing competition and lowering prices.

EXTENSION SERVICES AND TECHNICAL ASSISTANCE

It is not only because they are denied credit that women lack access to inputs that improve their yields and relieve some of their burden. The assistance provided by agricultural extension services, foreign aid and even NGOs may also be unavailable to them, because men are often seen as the farmers and household heads and women as the partners and helpers. Ruth Dixon argues thus:

The reluctance to 'see' women farmers comes not from their invisibility, but from a reluctance to share scarce resources with them.... Including women in labour force statistics in proportion to the amount of work they actually do is an essential first step in making female farmers visible to planners and policy makers.[32]

Where training and support services are directed specifically to women these are often in health, nutrition and home management rather than farming practice or technology.

A study by Kathleen Staudt of extension services and agricultural innovation in western Kenya found that in districts that had little contact with extension workers the productivity of men and women was about equal; in districts with extension workers the relative productivity of women had declined. Comparing farms that were similar in all respects except for the gender of their heads, Staudt found that farms with male heads were four times more likely to have been visited by an extension worker. She also found that 'capable

women were being ignored for non-innovative men'.[33]

A training programme in Thailand designed to improve dairy productivity was acknowledged to be a failure for the following reason: the men, who attended the course, could not retain enough of the information in enough detail to tell it to their wives, who were the ones who actually did the dairying.[34]

Initiatives for change The increasing understanding of the nature and extent of women's contribution to agricultural production is starting to be translated into policy, operational guidelines, and practice in the field. Approaches being used to ensure that extension services reach women farmers include:

- increasing the numbers of women in agricultural training;
- increasing the numbers of women extension workers;
- redesigning the curricula of agricultural training institutes;
- orienting extension services for women away from their home economics bias towards women's productive roles;
- training male extension workers to work directly with women farmers.[35]

In Indonesia and the Philippines about half the extension personnel are women; in Thailand one-quarter. Papua New Guinea has two hundred female extension officers, although the first women attended agricultural training college only in 1975. Eight regional centres for rural development have been established in Paraguay to provide services for women. Women's attendance at agricultural training institutions has increased in several African countries, and a training plan for women in agriculture as part of the National Agricultural

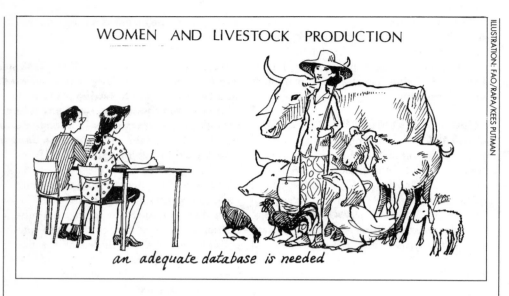

WOMEN AND LIVESTOCK PRODUCTION

an adequate database is needed

ILLUSTRATION: FAO/RAPA/KEES PUTMAN

Extension System is being put into practice in fifteen out of twenty-two states in India.[36]

A SUCCESSFUL CHILEAN SCHEME
Aware that the staff of the Institute of Rural Education (IER) in southeastern Chile had limited exposure to gender issues, UNIFEM decided to fund a course in gender-sensitization for IER staff before asking them to undertake a project with peasant women in a poor rural community in the Andes. The training module focuses on the need to listen to women and to understand the methods that enable families to survive with limited resources. The extension workers were advised that their project would probably fail if they attempted to impose ready-made 'solutions' on women who are already over-burdened. The women themselves would contribute to the design of the project through ongoing discussions. Although the module was developed for a particular project, it has been well received nationally as well as locally, and the Ministry of Agriculture plans to initiate its own training module for extension workers based on the participatory approach of the IER module.[37]

HEALTH AND SAFETY Increases in cash cropping, the removal of food subsidies, and reduced spending on services have put general health and nutritional standards at risk. Agricultural workers also suffer specific occupational health and safety hazards, mainly related to the use of pesticides and fungicides, but also to badly adapted machinery. Women's low bargaining power and the poor implementation of protective legislation in rural areas make them additionally vulnerable. Women are more likely to suffer from malnourishment but still have to carry heavy and awkward weights. Many of them work extremely long hours, which puts an additional strain on their systems, lowers resistance and causes stress. In such conditions, pregnancy and childbirth can be debilitating; lack of health services places them at further risk and adds the burden of caring for sick members of their household.

A World Health Organization (WHO) report on the occupational health of working women gives a strong warning on pesticides:

Without exception, pesticides are poisonous, and their use always involves the possibility of acute and chronic adverse effects on persons exposed to them. The special risk they present to women workers is a subject of major

concern to public health authorities because some of the chemicals employed are suspected to cause reproductive damage to women.[38]

The breast milk of women agricultural workers has been found to contain DDT, Dieldrin and Aldrin where these are used, and children only have to touch pesticide-contaminated clothing to get exposure levels that are too high.[39] The increasing numbers of women being drawn into waged work on commercial farms, where the use of chemicals is much greater than on smallholdings, means that more and more women are at risk in this way. Small-scale rural industries, too, are rarely covered by the health and safety standards, or the trade union monitoring, to which larger, urban factories would be subject.[40]

The Pesticides Action Network (PAN), based in Malaysia, provided information that has helped to curb the import by developing countries of some of the most hazardous pesticides. UNIFEM funded workshops in Indonesia, Malaysia and Thailand in 1991 on the theme of women and pesticides, part of a regional project initiated by the International Organization of Consumer Unions (IOCU) and coordinated by PAN.[41]

THE CHANGING RURAL LANDSCAPE

☐ The modernization process has been a two-edged sword. Whilst increased agricultural productivity is essential, so-called 'modernization' has not necessarily been the best way to achieve this. Pressures on countries to follow development policies based on growth and integration in the world economy have resulted in an emphasis on cash cropping, production for export, and mechanization which has not necessarily been conducive to widespread food security. One problem is the terms and conditions on which modernization measures have been introduced – often excluding small farmers, and women in particular. World trade also impacts on patterns of production: the narrow range of primary commodities that countries produce, the fluctuating but generally low prices they earn, and the dependence on Western markets all affect what is grown, where, how and by whom. At the same time, extensive subsidies for rich farmers, especially in the European Community (EC) and the United States, have led to overproduction there. This has resulted in the dumping of surpluses and lower prices for Third World farmers.[42]

CROPS FOR CASH AND EXPORT There

is nothing very new about cash cropping; cocoa, for example, was introduced into Ghana by the colonial administrators in the 1920s and 1930s. The earning of foreign exchange is such an important part of recent structural adjustment programmes, however, that for countries without a developed industrial sector the onus has been put on agricultural commodities and products, sometimes to the detriment of food production and consumption.

Increased production of cash crops has had mixed consequences. While employment opportunities are created on the one hand, many small farmers are losing land and becoming more dependent on wage labour. The increasing shortage of fertile land has sometimes resulted in a conflict of priorities: between cash and subsistence crops, between crops and livestock, between export and domestic production, and between men's and women's crops. In some countries, the combination of export-oriented production with cuts in food subsidies has had a disastrous impact: raising food prices and lowering nutrition levels. In Côte d'Ivoire a shortage of food staples resulted when the government encouraged men to grow cash crops, because they took over land used by the women for growing food, and diverted the women's labour to the cultivation of cash crops.

In a report on appropriate technology for rural women, UNIDO concluded that the intensive farming of cash crops has 'led to the creation of a two-sector division of the economy – traditional and modern – which is almost a two-sex division. The benefits accruing to men ... have often operated to move women to the very margin of subsistence'.[43] Women should not, however, be identified only with subsistence farming; many are engaged in cash cropping, on a full- or part-time basis, and many others would welcome the chance to diversify production and increase income in this way. On the basis of numerous projects the FAO has concluded that 'women are enthusiastic participants in market production, if they can participate on a fair basis alongside men'.[44]

NEW TECHNOLOGY Increasing production – whether of food or cash crops – may require certain technological inputs. It is now recognized, however, that the introduction of modern technology in situations of inequality in land and resources ownership runs the risk of making inequality worse. If yields go up for middle and larger landowners, this increases their wealth and also the gap between them and the many landless and land-poor. If a substantial proportion of the poor – small landholders and landless – rely on wage labour for a living, the introduction of mechanization may undermine and displace them. Labour-saving technologies could clearly be of benefit to women in many ways, but have often excluded them in practice.

The gender-specific dimension of technology becomes clear when one investigates who has access to improved seeds or technology, and on what terms. An ILO workshop on women and land in Africa heard examples from Tanzania, Mali and Niger of divergent interests and widening productivity gaps between men and women. More men have the opportunity to acquire new skills and to raise productivity through mechanization. Women, with less income, limited access to credit, and a secondary role in cash cropping, are particularly unlikely to be the beneficiaries of 'high-tech' government assistance or foreign aid packages. The fact that women's work is generally unpaid means that there is little market incentive to increase the productivity of their labour; it also means that they rarely have the resources to buy the technology themselves – or only limited access to a particular service such as milling or grinding. Most rural women also lack access to the basic infrastructure – the water, electricity, transport – which could lessen their reproductive burden and increase their productivity.

Women have not only been excluded from many benefits of technology, but they have also been negatively affected by its application. Mechanization has frequently displaced women from traditional tasks on which they relied for income. In Bangladesh, it is estimated that between 3.5 and 5 million work days per year would be needed to compensate female workers displaced by mechanized rice mills.[45] Aspects of technological change have also led to a greater burden on women: irrigation may permit double cropping, for example, or tractors may clear more land which then needs to be planted, weeded and harvested by women. As the improved fields are generally the men's, or 'family', plots, but rarely the women's, the women do not necessarily benefit from their increased workload. But the increased dependence of men on women's labour can sometimes work to women's advantage and give them some bargaining power. In Mauritania, the Gambia and Senegal it has resulted in women being paid by their husbands and other men in the village for transplanting and weeding, and for post-harvest tasks.[46]

The emphasis on the male farmer also means that women's special knowledge of many aspects of farming is ignored by the planners and experts, and is in danger of being lost. Ignoring women's experience has resulted in many mistakes in rural development. In Burkina Faso, for instance, irrigation and drainage canals designed by so-called 'experts', and built by village men with no experience of rice cultivation, led to over-drainage and aridity. In Côte d'Ivoire, new seed varieties were introduced which yield well but have very short stalks. As a result the women can no longer harvest with a sickle but must bend over using a small knife.[47]

INTRODUCING TECHNOLOGY IN AN APPROPRIATE MANNER Where technology, new or 'appropriate', is being introduced by government or humanitarian agencies, the onus is on them to make thorough and gender-specific studies of the possible consequences. The many NGOs involved in environmental issues and appropriate technology should review their own assumptions and practices, and take a lead in working with women to ensure that technology is, indeed, appropriate to both their productive and reproductive roles. There are, of course, many examples of good practice. In China, manual rice transplanters, fertilizer applicators, water pumps and grain-drying equipment have been introduced that save women's labour and increase their productivity but do not displace them from the agricultural process. In the Gambia, UNIFEM has provided milling machines to relieve women of the time-consuming job of pounding grain by hand.[48]

The question of who controls the technology must be addressed; there are many examples of men taking carts or machines that have been given to women. Women's access to new technology should be increased by extensive and focused training, and by employment policies that give preference to workers displaced by mechanization. When the processing of shea nuts in Mali was being mechanized, there were two options: a mill, which would result in total mechanization, and a press, which would leave some parts of the traditional process unchanged. The women concerned chose the press: in part because the technological jump was less great, and therefore less threatening, but also to protect their work from being taken over by men. The project reinforced the women's control by stipulating that all related tasks (administration, operation, maintenance) should be taken on by the women.[49]

CONCLUSION ☐ Most women in most rural areas have a tough time. Rural women have earlier marriages, more children and poorer health; both infant and maternal mortality are higher than in urban areas. School enrolments are lower in rural areas and illiteracy is higher. Rural women have poorer wages, more insecure employment, and longer hours of work. Customs and traditional practices often have a tighter hold; these may not all be to the disadvantage of women, but some directly threaten women's bodies, health, social status and freedom of movement. Forced and bonded labour is more common in rural areas. Isolation may be greater, because of distance, poor roads, and the lack of means even to buy a radio. Fewer workers are unionized, fewer public services and facilities are available, and fewer NGOs are active. These factors all impact on the quality of life, and make change more difficult to bring about.

The rural areas have consistently provided revenues which have in large part been spent on urban and industrial development. Governments need to decide whether the development of their country is best served by industry-led growth or by a new focus on agriculture and non-agricultural rural industry.[50] At present, the brightest rural young are still creamed off by the cities; new investment in rural industry and infrastructure, in tandem with equal opportunities for women in training and other services, could enhance development as well as increase women's participation in the process. There are signs that the spread of small towns and rural industries offers alternatives to some of the most exploitative feudal relationships, and to the growing poverty of women without land or income. It is argued that as households get closer to the market system, wives' labour becomes more important to their husbands. The outcome of the struggle between the sexes

over women's labour is not yet resolved, but a number of researchers believe that women's potential for leverage within the system is increasing.[51]

Key points to bear in mind for those planning and working with rural women are the need to make more use of women's knowledge and experience; to recognize differences of interest and responsibility in rural households; to raise public awareness about the role women play in agricultural production and resource management; and to use more participatory approaches, involving local women in decision making as well as implementation, and being open to learn from them.[52] The long-term objective must be both to increase women's control over the means of production and to reduce their multiple burdens.

1. Quoted in Commonwealth Secretariat, *Women, Conservation and Agriculture: a Manual for Trainers*, Commonwealth Secretariat, London, 1992.
2. United Nations Food and Agricultural Organization, quoted in 'Invisible farmers', *New Internationalist*, No. 149, 1985.
3. The overview that follows is largely based on *Rural Employment Promotion*, Report VII to the Seventy-fifth Session of the International Labour Conference, ILO, Geneva, 1988.
4. Zenebeworke Tadesse, 'Coping with change: an overview of women and the African economy', in Nancy O'Rourke (ed.), *The Future for Women in Development* (Proceedings of the Association for Women in Development Colloquium, Ottawa, 1990), North–South Institute.
5. Marilee Karl, 'Women and rural development', in *Women in Development: a Resource Guide for Organisation and Action*, ISIS/ITDG, London, 1991.
6. Audrey Bronstein, *The Triple Struggle*, War on Want, London, 1982, p. 67.
7. United Nations, *The World's Women: Trends and Statistics 1970–1990*, United Nations, New York, 1991, p. 82.
8. *WOMANKIND, Women, Livelihood and Production*, WOMANKIND Worldwide, London, n.d.
9. Ann Whitehead and Helen Bloom, 'Agriculture', in Lise Østergaard (ed.), *Gender and Development: a Practical guide*, Routledge, London and New York, 1992.
10. ILO, *Rural Employment Promotion*, p. 41.
11. Cecilia Ng, 'Malay women and rice production in West Malaysia', in Haleh Afshar (ed.), *Women, Development and Survival in the Third World*, Longman, London and New York, 1991.
12. WOMANKIND.
13. Bronstein.
14. WOMANKIND.
15. Richard Longhurst, 'Rural development planning and the sexual division of labour: a case study of a Moslem Hausa village in northern Nigeria', in ILO, *Rural

Development and Women in Africa*, ILO, Geneva, 1984.
16. ILO, *Women and Land* (report of a regional African workshop on women's access to land, October 1988, Zimbabwe), ILO, Geneva, 1989.
17. Society for Participatory Research in Asia (PRIA), *Creating Alternatives: Women and Work* (report of an Oxfam America-sponsored workshop), PRIA, New Delhi, 1987.
18. FAO, *Women, Food Systems, and Agriculture*, FAO, Rome, 1990, p. 7.
19. ILO, *Women and Land*.
20. Ibid.
21. Bina Agarwal, 'Gender relations and food security: coping with seasonality, drought and famine in South Asia', in Lourdes Beneria and Sally Feldman (eds), *Unequal Burden: Economic Crises, Persistent Poverty, and Women's Work*, Westview Press, Boulder and Oxford, 1992.
22. ILO, *Women and Land*.
23. FAO, *Food Systems*, pp. 23–24.
24. FAO, *Food Systems*.
25. ILO, *Women and Land*.
26. United Nations, *The World's Women*.
27. Ibid.
28. FAO, *Gender Issues in Rural Food Security in Developing Countries*, FAO, Rome, 1990, p. 8.
29. Ibid.
30. PRIA.
31. United Nations Industrial Development Organization (UNIDO), 'Women and human resource development for industry', UNIDO, Vienna, 1988.
32. FAO, *Food Systems*.
33. Whitehead and Bloom, p. 45.
34. FAO Regional Office for Asia and the Pacific (RAPA), *Women and Livestock Production*, RAPA, Bangkok, 1990.
35. FAO, *Food Systems*.
36. Ibid.
37. UNIFEM, *Annual Report 1991*, New York.
38. World Health Organization (WHO), Report of the

Expert Committee on Occupational Health for Working Women, WHO, Geneva, 1986, p. 35.

39. Alexandra Stephens, 'Decolonising agricultural information', FAO RAPA, Bangkok, n.d.

40. See Patricia Smyke, *Women and Health* and Annabel Rodda, *Women and the Environment* (both in Women and World Development Series), Zed Books, London, 1991, for further discussion of these and related issues.

41. UNIFEM.

42. Peter Madden, *A Raw Deal: Trade and the World's Poor*, Christian Aid, London, 1992.

43. UNIDO, 'Local production of appropriate technology for women', UNIDO, Vienna, 1989, p. 8.

44. ILO, *Women and Land*, p. 12.

45. FAO, *Food Systems*, p. 22.

46. Jennie Dey, *Women in Rice-farming Systems*, FAO, Rome, 1984.

47. Ibid.

48. Rodda.

49. UNIDO, 'Appropriate technology'.

50. Alexandra Stephens, 'Sustainable agricultural development and poverty alleviation', FAO RAPA, Bangkok, 1992.

51. Whitehead and Bloom.

52. Commonwealth Secretariat, p. 17.

4 THE INFORMAL SECTOR: LAST RESORT OR ENGINE OF GROWTH?

Women in informal projects do not 'supplement' wage earnings.... If anything, the salary at the end of the month supplements the small businesses.... Women's economic interactions, however small-scale and petty they may appear, have in the case of Tanzania proven to be the backbone sustaining entire urban populations in the face of industrial decline.[1]

THE DIVERSITY OF ACTIVITIES in the informal sector makes it difficult to define, and their connections with 'formal' manufacture, services and agriculture make it hard to draw clear boundaries. The informal sector is especially important in developing countries but exists in most industrialized countries too. While providing much urban employment it is also part of the rural environment. Activities are generally 'own-account' but they may also be part of a subcontracting chain. One firm, even one workplace, can span the formal and informal sectors, employing both a regular workforce and casual workers, as well as outworkers. One person may work in both the informal and formal sectors in the course of a day.

What is clear is that informal activities make an enormous and, in many countries, increasing contribution to the incomes of households and nations. Indeed, in spite of the status of the formal, 'modern' sector, falling real wages in the course of the 1980s and since means that it provides only a peripheral source of income for many people. It is also clear that as informal activities have expanded so – in the great majority of countries – has women's share in them.

DEFINING 'INFORMAL' □ During the 1960s the idea took shape among researchers and planners that outside the modern, organized, 'visible' sector of work lay another sector: here, people unable to get 'proper' work engaged in a variety of largely traditional activities in order to sustain themselves. This was the concept of informal work as failure (in terms of industrialization) and marginal (in terms of its contribution to the economy), an idea that has since been challenged but nevertheless persists, as does the modern/traditional dichotomy.

In 1972, in the context of an employment mission to Kenya, the ILO introduced the concept of 'informal sector', defining its main characteristics as:

- ease of entry
- reliance on local resources
- family ownership of enterprises
- small-scale operations
- labour-intensive work, using adaptive technologies
- the use of skills acquired outside schooling
- an irregular and competitive market.

A new idea was that the sector had untapped development potential, and later concepts – especially in the face of stagnating growth and rising unemployment – have stressed the idea of the informal sector as opportunity rather than failure, a manifestation of 'natural' entrepreneurial qualities which, if promoted, could kick-start the development process.

Bodies such as the ILO and the United Nations Statistical Office have attempted to refine the definition of the informal sector, with the aim of developing national statistics that can be compared over time and between countries. The 'own-account' nature of most informal employment is often stressed, although other analysts identify a spectrum of employment relations, from self-employment to both disguised and 'true' but insecure wage work.[2] The fact that most informal units are not registered (that is, they are outside national accounting, labour legislation, and social protection) has become part of some definitions, and it is also used to explain the sector's greater capacity to provide employment. The informal sector has thus been likened to a 'safety net' for workers without regular employment or social security and to a 'sponge' which absorbs surplus labour.

Contrasts abound in terms of occupations and employment relations, and so do divisions on the basis of access to resources and of gender. Gita Sen, in *INSTRAW News*, distinguishes between people whose goal is growth and expansion, those simply seeking stability and security, and those for whom the informal sector is their last chance of survival. As she says, 'some distinction needs to be made between the woman handcart puller who pulls loads on the city streets and the small entrepreneur who produces and sells garments for export'.[4]

IS THE CONCEPT VALID? An increasing number of commentators and activists argue that the informal sector is not only linked to the formal sector but is part of it.[5] Clearly, many informal activities are directly linked to both the consumption and the production of the so-called formal sector. The word 'sector' may be as misleading as 'informal', as it conveys ideas of a specific location rather than a spectrum of activities and strategies, and of separation from other facets of life, including the domestic sphere.

Others challenge the whole concept. At a workshop on the informal sector, participants from developing countries raised fundamental questions:

- Can something which makes up over half the economic life of a city be called 'informal'?

- Is the informal sector not a Western concept, based on the belief that industrial production and waged labour are, or should be, the norm?

- Is the sector viewed as informal because

ROLE OF THE INFORMAL SECTOR

The informal sector provides goods and services for millions of people, as well as employment. A United Nations Development Programme (UNDP) handbook on informal sector activities in Africa stresses the invaluable contribution they make to social and economic life in Africa by:

- job creation, generating nearly ten times more jobs than the formal sector in the course of the 1980s;

- contributing to GDP: some 25 per cent in Nigeria, for example;

- training through on-the-job experience and informal apprenticeships;

- self-help social services, from credit schemes to schools and community centres;

- linkages with other sectors: providing goods and services to, and obtaining them from, agriculture and manufacturing.[3]

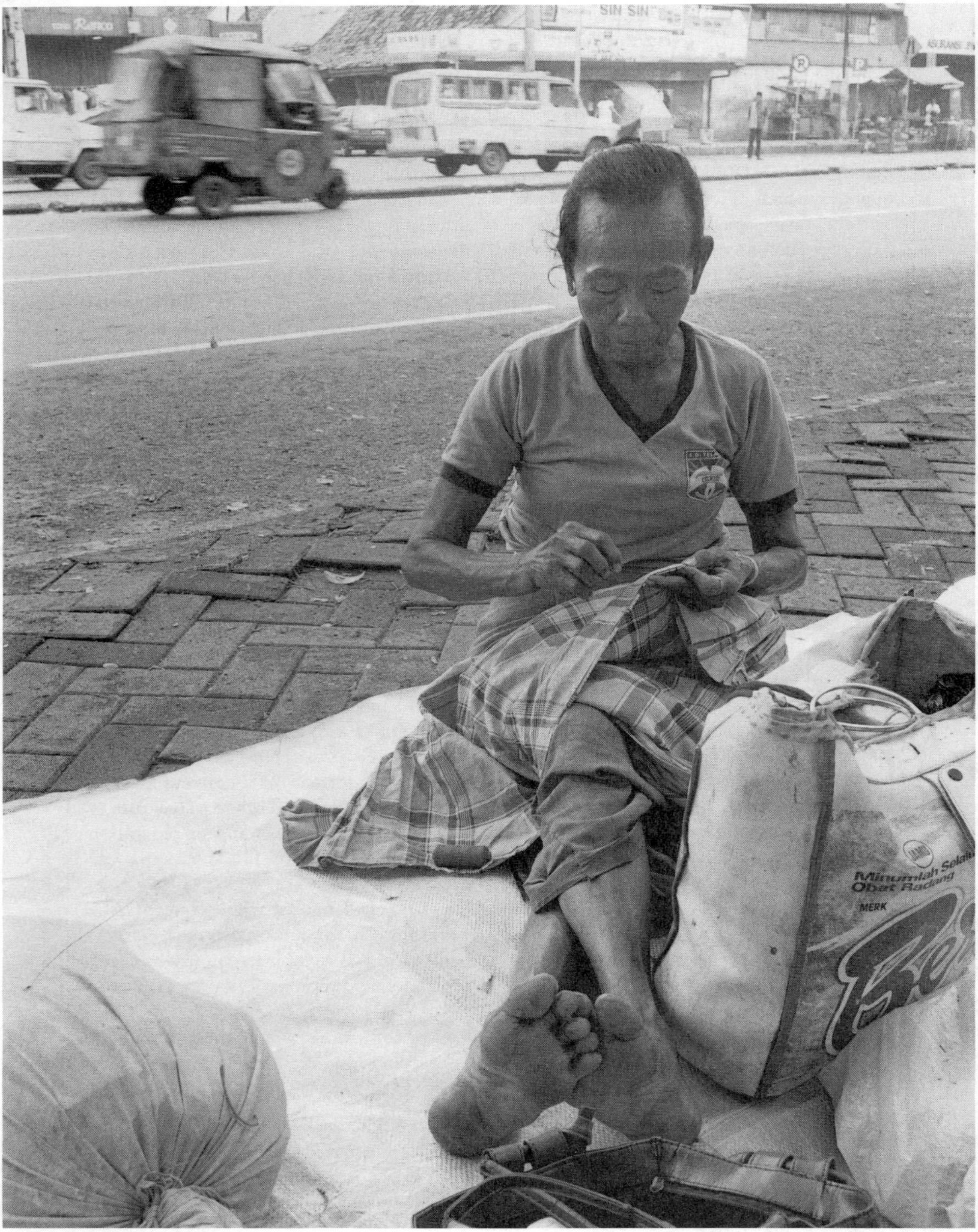

PHOTO: ILO/J. MAILLARD

Sewing on a Jakarta pavement

it provides employment for so many women?

- Do women struggling for survival see their own labour as informal?[6]

The Self-Employed Women's Association (SEWA) works to protect and organize women in the informal sector in India, but consciously avoids the 'informal' designation. By using the term 'self-employment' it seeks to emphasize the fact that women are workers and to enhance their dignity.[7]

WHERE IS THE INFORMAL SECTOR?

Just as the informal sector links into the formal, so informal activities are part of the rural as well as the urban economy, and they connect at many points. On the one hand, many rural–urban distinctions are quite artificial, and there is constant movement between the two. Rural and urban areas interact as producers and consumers: much trading and processing relies on supplies from rural areas, of food, for example, while remittances from towns help to sustain rural communities. Trading may be outside the cash economy: in Jamaica, fresh vegetables and country produce may be exchanged for manufactured goods, often within kinship networks.[8] On the other hand, much agriculture is itself an informal activity, in that many farmers are own-account or casual labourers outside the reach of laws, social protection or labour organization. Many non-farm activities, too, are conducted on an informal basis and resemble the sorts of projects women start up in urban areas: trading, preparing food for sale, and handicrafts.

Some agencies deliberately exclude agriculture from definitions of the informal sector, and statistics on it, on the grounds that agricultural statistics are quite distinct from non-agricultural, that the outputs of agriculture tend to be similar, and that different methodological approaches are needed.[9] Better statistics and more studies are also needed and, as C.K. Omari argues, the informal sector should in any case be taken into account in strategies for rural development.[10]

GROWTH AND CHANGE IN INFORMAL EMPLOYMENT

☐ If defining the informal sector presents difficulties so does measuring it, though it is clearly growing in many countries in the face of stagnant or contracting employment opportunities in both manufacturing and agriculture. In Africa, the informal sector employs an estimated 61 per cent of the urban labour force, and is expected to generate around 93 per cent of new jobs in the urban areas in the 1990s.[11] Asia is a particularly diverse region; while growth has been maintained by the four NIEs (Singapore, South Korea, Taiwan and Hong Kong), manufacturing employment has slowed in South Asia, and most countries still have serious problems of unemployment and poverty. The 1992 *World Labour Report* estimated that while the organized sector grew at about 2 per cent a year through the 1980s, the urban informal sector managed 4 per cent and more, providing between 40 and 66 per cent of urban employment, depending on the country. In Latin America, debt and structural adjustment resulted in a rise in the poverty rate from 35 per cent of the population in 1980 to 44 per cent in 1990. The proportion of workers in the informal sector rose by 56 per cent in the course of the 1980s, while total non-agricultural employment rose by 30 per cent.[12]

Another key factor in the growth of informal activity in most developing regions has been the plummeting value of wages. In the first half of the 1980s, the purchasing power of the minimum wage fell by 40 per cent in Kenya and 80 per cent in Sierra Leone.[13] By 1990, the minimum wage in Bolivia, Ecuador and Paraguay was one-third of its 1980 value.

PHOTO: FAO/J. VAN ACKER

Marketing: one of the most widespread of women's businesses

In Tanzania in 1976, wages made up nearly 80 per cent of total household income, but by 1988 they provided only 10 per cent of income; in 1988 one worker's monthly salary could buy three days' food for six people.[14] Thus, the informal sector has not only offered the possibility of work to the unemployed, but has permitted the survival of many households with wage earners. The extent to which governments, too, have come to rely on the informal sector was demonstrated in a speech by Tanzania's President Mwinyi on May Day 1990: 'No salary increase would enable us to meet all requirements.... Therefore, I would like to repeat my appeal to fellow workers to initiate small projects which would supplement their income.'[15]

A growing informal sector exists in industrialized countries too, though nei-ther the scale nor conditions should be lightly compared with those in developing countries. On the one hand is the parallel economy – often called 'moonlighting' – stimulated by falling wages and fear for the future. Most people work on their own account, sometimes in addition to formal employment: men may drive a taxi in the evenings or do car repairs; women may clean houses or mind children. On the other hand there is the 'informalization' of labour: rising numbers of workers are employed on irregular or undeclared con-tracts, and it is of particular significance that a great majority of them are women and migrants. Homeworking is one face of the informal sector in industrialized coun-tries, though it is also one of the principal lines of connection between the formal and informal sectors (see below).

The informal sector did not form part of the ideology of the centrally planned economies, though in practice the system was largely maintained by an informal 'exchange sector'. The current strains on the economies of former socialist countries are resulting in massive poverty and unemployment. The informal sector is growing but also changing, as the system of contacts on which exchange was based has broken down in the course of political and economic restructuring. Its public face is the city streets lined with people selling their few remaining possessions, or surplus supplies from factories and regiments that are being dismantled.

THE DIVISION OF LABOUR ☐ Some division of labour exists between formal and informal sectors on the basis of gender. The extent to which the informal sector is a 'female' sector varies geographically and over time, especially as unemployment rises; nevertheless, in most countries women's possibilities for entering the formal sector remain even more limited than men's, and the informal sector may be their only option – not simply the last resort.

It has been suggested that for men the informal sector is a stopgap until they find formal employment, whilst women tend to stay within it.[16] This is not necessarily because of a lack of choice; for some women, the flexibility of working arrangements and diversity of opportunities are the positive side of informal activity.

In the course of the 1980s, as more and more men lost their jobs, or falling wages and rising prices made their incomes inadequate, or families split up through migration or divorce, women were drawn into own-account work or wage labour on whatever terms they could get. 'You can't wait for your husband to bring home money,' said a woman interviewed in Tanzania. Another explained, 'Women are

trying their best. They are affected most by the hardships and want to see the well-being of their children. It is their responsibility to the family.'[17]

WHAT PEOPLE DO A sexual division of labour, reinforced by poverty, also exists within the informal sector. Women in self-employment rely on the skills and experience they already have, and so food processing and trading, sewing, domestic and personal services, are all important. Women's domestic responsibilities force them to turn either their homes into a workplace or their place of work into a home: small children may spend more time under their mother's market stall than in their homes, slightly older children become part of the labour force.

A DAY'S TRADING
Georgina gets up at 4.30 a.m., dresses, then wakes her eldest daughter to say she is leaving. She goes first to a private moneylender to borrow the equivalent of $4, then to the bus station where a range of agricultural produce is being sold by people with smallholdings in the country areas. She buys enough vegetables to fill two baskets then walks to a more central part of the town. She sits by the side of the road and offers the vegetables for sale. After a couple of hours a policeman comes along, kicks over one of the baskets, and tells her to move on. She moves to another spot, and in the course of the day manages to sell most of the vegetables. She goes back to the moneylender and pays him $5. She goes home and cooks the rest of the vegetables in a stew for her family.

Women are especially numerous in the lowest-paid and most exploited categories of work: in small enterprises where they may work in sweatshop conditions or as outworkers; in the simplest types of self-employment, with minimal capital, tools, and raw materials; as unpaid family workers; in domestic work; and in commercial sex work. The range of jobs women perform is as limited in the informal sector as it is everywhere. It is not that women lack

PHOTO: ILO/J. MAILLARD

Turning the workplace into a home: selling on a Lima street

initiative or business ability; on the contrary, the way women are able to scrape an income together on the basis of almost no inputs but their own labour and ingenuity inspires admiration and respect. But when the margins are too tight, it is almost impossible to turn survival activities into growth.

With a small amount of capital women have often done very well; in one family the husband, a welder, gave his wife enough money to start a project making and selling *mbege*, a drink made from bananas. Within a year she was earning twenty-six times her husband's wage. Although such disparities can cause problems in the household, men surveyed in Dar es Salaam supported their wives' projects because they saw they had no choice. They might have liked to object 'but they keep quiet. They know they can't support the family and they need the women's income.'[18] The women interviewed said that what they gained in freedom, and relief from money worries, was worth any trouble their husbands gave. The shift in household relations, and women's sense of their place in society, has been considerable.

HOMEWORKING ☐ Homeworking takes place not only in the informal sector. It is a common form of employment in both rural and urban areas, and in industrialized as well as developing countries. Frequently the last stage in a subcontracting chain, homeworking may be directly connected with manufacturing and even services, but at the same time it often takes place on terms and conditions that must be considered informal. Some 90 per cent of homeworkers are women.

Homeworking was the basis of much pre-industrial economic activity in the developed regions, and it also made an important contribution to the early stages of industrialization. Many people find it diffi-cult to believe that it still exists on any substantial scale, or they associate it with traditional craft-based tasks. As van Luijken and Mitter say, however:

It is the hands of the home-workers that produce a large variety of the goods we buy in the markets of the West: toys, rugs, garments, lampshades ... and many other products [including] the components for high-tech industries.[19]

THE RISE IN HOMEWORKING In the last part of the twentieth century, homeworking has both increased and become more visible and discussed – largely thanks to research and action by homeworkers and concerned activists. The increase has in part reflected changes in the organization of work: as production processes have fragmented, work has been contracted to smaller units of production, thus giving employers greater flexibility but reducing the protection of workers. A homeworker is of course the smallest unit of all, and the most vulnerable.

Homeworking has also increased because of growing pressure on women to contribute to the family income. Many women need to earn money in ways that neither challenge the male breadwinner ethos, nor leave undone their domestic responsibilities. The lack of child care, in particular, ties many women to the home. Alison Lever, writing about a village in Spain where most women embroider for a living in their homes – and earn a substantial part of the family wage – quotes a male entrepreneur: '[Embroidering is] not proper work, because it is done in a woman's free time, between tending to her children.'[20] Mitter quotes a homeworker she interviewed: '[The family] doesn't object to me working as long as I can be home to get their tea.'[21]

Bosses do not object to women working either, so long as they accept low wages and poor conditions of work. Employers

PHOTO: ANNEKE VAN LUIJKEN

Homeworkers usually earn less than the minimum wage

benefit from women's lack of choice and the undervaluing of their skills. It is important to recognize that a number of women work at home on their own account – offering a service or running a small business – but many more work on a piece-rate basis.

RACISM AND HOMEWORKING

Depending on economic circumstances, migrant workers may be seen as a convenient reserve of labour or as 'out to get our jobs'. Structures that divide working people are fed by myths and stereotypes, among them the idea that migrant and immigrant women are culturally bound to the home, make no effort to adapt to the 'host' country and its work patterns, do not speak the language – so they prefer homeworking. The reality is that they are forced into the home by the same structural factors

ADVANTAGES TO EMPLOYERS USING HOMEWORKERS

- Labour costs are lower, not just direct wages but social costs such as health insurance, maternity leave and so on.

- Capital investment, in space or machinery, is minimal (with the exception of a small amount of work using information technology/teleworking).

- Overheads, such as electricity, cleaning and so on, are paid by the workers.

- They can ignore regulations, such as health and safety standards, which apply to workplaces.

- The risks of union activity, and collective action or demands, are minimal because the workers are so dispersed.

- Many employers have no contact with, and even less responsibility for, their workers as they act through one or several agents.

as other women, with the additional oppression of discrimination on the basis of race. A survey carried out among Asian women in London provides a good illustration of the reality as opposed to the myth:

- All but one of the homeworkers had had labour market experience, but one-third had been made redundant and were subsequently unable to find jobs.

- A significant proportion of the women had left their outside job because of intolerable levels of racial and sexual harassment.

- One-third had given up their jobs when they became pregnant, though not because husbands or mothers-in-law insisted on it: the reason was simply the lack of child care.[22]

In an interview with Swasti Mitter, a Bangladeshi woman in London talked about the numbers of racist attacks on Asians and asked: 'How can I look for jobs outside my home in such a situation? I want to remain invisible, literally.' Her uncle brings machine work to her home and although the pay is low, 'I earn, and feed my children somehow. Most of all, I do not have to deal with the fear of racist abuse in this white world.'[23]

LEGISLATION A growing number of laws relate specifically to homeworkers, but enforcement is particularly difficult.[26] Other labour laws effectively exclude homeworkers by applying narrow definitions of work and workplace or conditions that rule them out. The abuses of the homeworking system have led to calls for its abolition, but most policy-makers and activists recognize the need of many women for this type of work and the lack of alternatives. Recent years have seen a range of efforts to bring some form of reg-

TWO HOMEWORKERS

Julie (Malaysia): 'I work at home like my mother did, and most of the members of my [Indian] community. We make the paper "money" used in Chinese funeral ceremonies. I am 22, I have two young children, and I mainly work in the evenings, often until after midnight. I left school when I was fifteen and worked in a local factory until I got married. I am glad to have a paid job I can do at home; my husband is a labourer and I provide about a third of the family's income. I worry that I have no sickness or unemployment protection, and I often get backache and sore eyes. I have spoken with other women doing the same work and we plan to ask for better rates of pay.'[24]

Amarjit (United Kingdom): 'I have certifi-

cates in computing, but I decided to start working in my home; if I went out to work, I'd have to pay the childminder a fortune for two small children. I used to overlock sweatshirts, pyjamas, children's clothes, etc. For most factories, outworkers sew only parts of a garment, but in my case I had to sew complete garments from start to finish. When you're working at home no one gives you the right wages, hours of work, holidays, etc. It's always more and more [work] they want. I was doing 100 sweatshirts per day, sometimes more, but the employers said that I was not doing enough, they even told me not to bother taking my eldest son to nursery school, as it was wasting time! I worked 15 hours a day, sometimes more.

Hardly surprisingly I fell ill and was unable to sew.'[25]

ulation to the sector and thus, it is hoped, an improvement of conditions.[27] Home-workers themselves have taken action to set up local groups and meetings to exchange information and increase their bargaining power. SEWA in India was instrumental both in gaining recognition for homeworkers in national legislation, and in getting the international trade union movement to take up the issue. NGOs, trade unions, the European Commission and the ILO have all taken action to investigate the scale of homeworking, identify the particular problems involved, and develop a practical response.

Measures include making provisions in national legislation, registering both home-workers and employers, and raising public awareness. An important principle is that obligations should be imposed on the firms which ultimately profit from the home-workers' labour, whether these are the direct employer or not. They would have responsibility for the working conditions of the individual homeworker and for the actions of their agents. Pressure has also been brought to bear on the ILO to produce a standard on the social protection of homeworking, and it looks likely that this will happen in the near future.

The Hong Kong Association of Women Workers gives special priority to homeworkers, who are extremely numerous. They campaign around child care facilities, pay and conditions and, in particular, health and safety, as a survey found that a quarter of homeworkers had suffered a work-related injury. The women's trade union in the Netherlands, Vrouwenbond FNV, has set up three regional homeworkers' support centres. These aim to improve the situation of individual workers through information, advice and contact while campaigning for long-term improvements for homeworkers in general.[28]

REGULATING THE INFORMAL SECTOR AND PROMOTING EMPLOYMENT ☐

The strategies adopted by those planning for this sector differ sharply depending on whether they see it as a 'safety net' or as an 'engine for growth'. 'There is a lot of dynamism in the informal sector, and women are the most important part of [it].... In Africa, when you talk about indigenous small enterprise, you are really talking about women,' says Henri Bazin of UNDP.[29] On the other hand, Gita Sen warns, 'If it is the petty self-employed segment that has been growing during the last decade, then the optimism regarding the growth potential of the surge in informal activities may be excessive, if not misplaced.'[30] One view is not necessarily right at the expense of the other: the diversity of the informal sector is readily acknowledged. And though women are particularly vulnerable in a number of ways, their strengths must not be overlooked, neither must their role in distributing resources through the household. Policy-makers and donors have much to learn from their coping strategies.

Maria Otero of Accion International, which provides credit and training to thousands of micro-entrepreneurs in Latin America, calls for developers to reach out to those beneath the informal sector pyramid, to the pre-entrepreneurs who have been largely overlooked to date:

The danger is that development agencies will gravitate to the top of the pyramid where pay-offs are likely to be quicker. Only a tiny fraction of the sector is currently receiving any resources.... There is a whole urban mass being left out.[31]

It is harder to reconcile calls to regulate the informal sector (introducing registration and standards to protect workers) with arguments that the sector should be unregulated in order to encourage ease of entry and entrepreneurship. The particular vulnerability of workers outside the reach of labour legislation or the trade union movement is neither an acceptable nor a necessary price to pay for informal employment opportunities. Another question regards the extent to which the informal sector is linked to, even determined by, the formal sector. Can the informal sector mop up excess labour indefinitely, or will it contract and fail if growth does not pick up in the formal sector? All the indications are that the informal sector is not infinitely elastic; employment opportunities may even decrease in parallel with opportunities in the formal sector. The importance of structural factors is demonstrated by the fact that the transition from self-employment to small enterprise is found to be more difficult in Africa than in Latin America,[32] and is everywhere more difficult for women than for men.

There is general agreement about the importance of a better understanding of own-account, household-based, micro-entrepreneurial activities, and the relationships between them. To improve the situation of African women in the informal sector, the UNDP is funding a $2.7 million inter-agency project, which strongly emphasizes defining, measuring and understanding the sector before intervening. Its long-term goal is to make women's activities more productive in three key sectors: manufacturing, trade, and services. Its strategy concentrates on statistics, policy development, and training. The United Nations International Research and Training Institute for the Advancement of Women (INSTRAW) has a key role, being responsible for the development of concepts and methodology, as well as training, in relation to the statistical component. Four countries have been chosen for the initial case studies: Burkina Faso, Congo, the Gambia, and Zambia.[33]

CREDIT AND TRAINING The diverse occupations, ambitions, and needs of people working 'informally' mean that the programmes designed to reach them will also have to adopt a range of strategies. The links between formal and informal activities mean that programmes based on movement between the two make more sense than a separate strategy for the informal sector alone.[34] Both training and credit, together and separately, are seen as ways of increasing women's productive capabilities and bargaining power. There can, however, be differences in emphasis.

Because so many women are coming into the informal sector in Africa from the same base of unskilled activities, UNIFEM's Marilyn Carr believes that diversification is the key:

Credit is not the answer. If women have no skills, or are all doing the same thing and have no market, different techniques of production are required, and not just handing out credit. It's more a question of linkages than funding; women with a background or interest in a particular occupation need to be linked up with training centres and national women's machineries.[35]

Maria Otero, however, although her organization provides training, believes that technical skills are not enough:

Many people in the informal sector already have considerable trade skills, and those that don't cannot afford the luxury of waiting to be trained.... Opening up access to capital, [thus increasing] women's leverage, may be necessary before concentrating on skills training.[36]

Jana Everett and Mira Savara undertook an evaluation of the impact of credit on petty commodity producers in India. They found that the loans which have the most positive impact are those made within a framework of other activities designed to replace existing exploitative

TRIBUNE

PROBLEM SOLVING

IDENTIFYING AND FINDING SOLUTIONS FOR YOUR MARKETING PROBLEMS

relations of production and to improve productive capacity. These include: the creation of collective workplaces; unified action to oppose harassment by officials and others; lobbying for policy changes; and, especially, the creation of a forum for discussion, problem solving and collective action. 'The real issue is not women's organizations making the loan programmes work but, instead, the loan programme facilitating organizational development among women petty commodity producers.'[37] These findings are borne out by the experience of such well-established bodies as the Grameen Bank in Bangladesh, where credit is one plank of the organizing strategy, and conversely by the lack of success of government schemes, pitched at the individual, in reaching the poorest. (See, too, the description of the Working Women's Forum in Chapter 8.)

CONCLUSION □ In this chapter we have seen examples both of pressures on women, reinforcing their responsibilities for feeding the family, and of new opportunities, new freedoms, and new power – even for some of the poorest women. How does the positive balance against the negative, and what are the possibilities for deeper and more lasting change? One conclusion is offered by Aili Mari Tripp, who worked with self-employed women in the suburbs of Dar es Salaam:

Although it is too early to say how or whether women's expanding economic role will translate into political leverage or other forms of power and influence, the implications of these changes in the household economy have not been lost on men, or on women for that matter. Gender relations and perceptions are clearly in flux.[38]

The challenge now is to build on these possibilities. Solutions need to be as various as the needs, and programmes must be based on a sound understanding of local conditions and, above all, of the outlook and priorities of the people concerned. One important element is the collection of data that give a fuller picture of women's many activities, and an analysis of the constraints on their participation. Another is the creation of a broad 'enabling' environment through the reform of laws and the development of positive public policies. These should encourage innovative and comprehensive employment promotion strategies, which include: motivating and guiding female entrepreneurs; improving their access to credit, skills and facilities; and making links with markets, larger enterprises, and the formal sector in general. Employment promotion also needs to be linked in an integrated way with social protection policies. The powerlessness and isolation experienced by many women working in informal and home-based activities should be addressed through group formation and organization.[39]

1. Aili Mari Tripp, 'The impact of crisis and economic reform on women in urban Tanzania', in Lourdes Benería and Shelley Feldman (eds), *Unequal Burden: Economic Crises, Persistent Poverty and Women's Work*, Westview Press, Boulder and Oxford, 1992, p. 174.
2. Noeleen Heyzer, 'Women, Subsistence and the Informal Sector: Towards a Framework of Analysis', Discussion Paper 163, Institute of Development Studies, Sussex, 1981.
3. United Nations Development Programme (UNDP), *Supporting Informal Sector Activities of African Women*, UNDP, New York, n.d.
4. Gita Sen, 'Capturing the elusive concept of "informal sector"', in *Women and Development*, double issue of *INSTRAW News*, No. 16, 1991, p. 9.
5. See, for example, Sallie Westwood, 'Gender and the politics of production in India', in Haleh Afshar (ed.), *Women, Development and Survival in the Third World*, Longman, Harlow, 1991.
6. International Restructuring Education Network Europe (IRENE), *Women as Workers: Report of International Seminar on the Informalization of Women's Labour*, IRENE, Tilburg, 1986.
7. Westwood.
8. Helen I. Safa and Peggy Antrobus, 'Women and the economic crisis in the Caribbean', in Benería and Feldman (eds).
9. 'Why agriculture is left out', in *Women and Development*, double issue of *INSTRAW News*, No. 16, 1991.
10. C.K. Omari, *Rural Women, Informal Sector and Household Economy in Tanzania*, UNU/WIDER, Helsinki, 1989.
11. ILO, *World Labour Report*, 1992.
12. *The Dilemma of the Informal Sector*: report of the Director-General to the Seventy-eighth Session of the International Labour Conference, ILO, Geneva, 1991.
13. ILO, *World Labour Report*, 1993.
14. Tripp.
15. Ibid., p. 173.
16. ILO/UNDP, *A Comprehensive Women's Employment Strategy for Indonesia*, ILO Regional Office for Asia and the Pacific, Bangkok, 1993.
17. Tripp, p. 167.
18. Ibid., p. 171.
19. Anneke van Luijken and Swasti Mitter, *Unseen Phenomenon: the Rise of Homeworking*, Change, London, n.d., p. 3.
20. Alison Lever, 'Capital, gender and skill: women homeworkers in rural Spain', *Feminist Review*, No. 30, 1988.
21. Swasti Mitter, *Common Fate, Common Bond: Women in the Global Economy*, Pluto Press, London, 1986, p. 119.
22. IRENE, 'Not a proper job', report of international conference on homeworking, *News from IRENE*, No. 12, 1990.
23. Mitter, p. 130.
24. IRENE, 'Not a proper job'.
25. Case study from education materials produced by the Leicester Outwork Campaign.
26. Luz Vega Ruiz, 'Home work: towards a new regulatory framework?', *International Labour Review*, Vol. 131, No. 2, 1992.
27. ILO, *Conditions of Work Digest*, Vol. 8, No. 2, 1989.
28. IRENE, 'Not a proper job'.
29. Quoted in editorial in *Women and Development*, double issue of *INSTRAW News*, No. 16, 1991.
30. Sen.
31. 'Rethinking the informal sector: an interview with Maria Otero', in *Grassroots Development*, Vol. 13, No. 1, 1989, p. 8.
32. ILO, *World Labour Report*, 1992.
33. 'INSTRAW project on informal sector in Africa attempts new statistical breakthrough', in *INSTRAW News*, No. 16, 1991.
34. UNIDO, *Human Resources in Zimbabwe's Industrial Development: the Current and Prospective Contribution of Women*, United Nations Industrial Development Organization, Vienna, 1989.
35. 'INSTRAW ... attempts new statistical breakthrough', p. 3.
36. 'Interview with Maria Otero', p. 5.
37. Jana Everett and Mira Savara, 'Institutional credit as a strategy towards self-reliance for petty commodity producers in India: a critical evaluation', in Afshar (ed.), pp. 240, 255.
38. Tripp, p. 170.
39. See discussion in ILO/UNDP, *Women's Employment ... Indonesia*.

5 INDUSTRIAL EMPLOYMENT: FREEDOM OR NEW EXPLOITATION?

Modern industry offers an important vehicle for accelerating [women's participation] insofar as in its own development it tends to challenge traditional structures and values in many ways.[1]

THE MODERN MANUFACTURING SECTOR has grown unevenly in different developing countries, depending on a range of factors, from the availability of raw materials and labour to political stability and the level of foreign investment. The reasons for success have not always been clear, and disagreement is intense over the relative importance of internal factors, especially government policy, and external factors, especially international investment and trade.

The extent of women's participation has also varied: at different stages and in different regions, women have been both excluded from and exploited by industrial development.[2] Asia is the only region in the world where women's employment share is higher in industry than in services, and the numbers of women in industrial employment in that continent exceed those in Africa and Latin America combined. In all regions, however, their numbers have been growing; between 1960 and 1980 the proportion of women employed in the industrial sector almost doubled in the developing countries.[3] The industrialization process has not been limited to the growth of local manufacturing; a major factor was the relocation of industries from developed to developing countries from the 1960s on.

THE FIRST RESTRUCTURING: 'RUN-AWAY' CAPITAL ☐ The second half of the twentieth century has seen the rise of businesses that set up production in many countries, invest in many more, have turnovers greater than the national budget of some countries, are beyond the control of most national and international legislation, and buy from and sell to themselves through extensive networks of subsidiaries: the transnational corporations (TNCs).

In the course of the 1950s and 1960s, the standardization and mass production of many components led to sharp competition in pricing. At the same time wages, employment levels, and working conditions improved in the industrialized countries, strengthening the position of workers in relation to employers. TNCs started to look further afield both for markets and for sources of labour. The first phase of international restructuring was based on the relocation of production to parts of the world where economic and social conditions made labour cheap and apparently easy to manipulate. The industries concerned were those with a high labour content and a relatively low level of mechanization, which are also those traditionally employing large numbers of women. So, in a number of countries, a whole new population – young, mainly unmarried women – was brought into the labour force for the first time.

The restructuring of production was made possible by developments in technology – especially information processing and communications technology – that

70

PHOTO: ILO

The high numbers of women in industrial employment in Asia: Japanese television factory

71

made geographical distance almost disappear. Returns were well worth the investment. While average rates of return on manufacturing investment in the USA fell from 15.5 to under 10 per cent between 1966 and 1974, returns of between 50 and 400 per cent were 'no problem' to maintain in some Third World countries, according to an assistant to the president of one US-based global corporation.[4]

FLEXIBILIZATION: THE NEW RESTRUCTURING □ As growth faltered
both in national economies and in international trade in the course of the 1970s, further restructuring measures were taken in an attempt to halt the decline and to reestablish profitability. A key idea was 'flexibilization': in product ranges, in output, in organization, in technology and – especially – in the use of labour. The purpose was to respond rapidly and effectively to market changes; the 'competitive edge' of a company is more often gained or lost at this point than in the course of production.

Labour flexibility means that a smaller proportion of workers are a fixed overhead and long-term responsibility of the company: these are the 'core' workers – managerial and technical staff – who are usually male. Other workers, considered to be unskilled, are hired as needed on short-term contracts. More and more processes are automated, or subcontracted: in many industries there has been an increasing duality as factories modernize while the jobs that remain labour-intensive are put out. Women workers are often used as a low-cost substitute for mechanization.[5] This may be seen in the textile industries of India, Hong Kong and the United Kingdom, the electronics industry in the USA and the Netherlands, the car industry in Italy. An Italian professor of engineering once said, 'Women make the most flexible robots of all' – a reference to car advertisements that boasted: 'hand-made by robots.'[6]

The declining importance of labour (or at least 'unskilled' labour) and the growing importance of a flexible response to the market have resulted in a certain degree of relocation 'back North'; where production processes are being put out internationally, they are increasingly skill-intensive. The hunt is now on for cheap skilled labour.[7]

The industrialization avenue of many developing countries in the sixties and seventies based on low-skill manufacturing for exports may become an increasingly narrow path in future.... This implies that unless the prevailing occupational gender stereotypes – assigning low skill jobs to women – can be changed, the latter stand to lose whatever the outcome may be: either by reduced inflow of foreign investment or by changing skill requirements which currently only a minority of female workers are able to meet.[8]

THE IMPACT OF INTERNATIONAL RESTRUCTURING □ It is important to
get a perspective on the scale of transnational operations. Valentine Moghadam rightly points out that 'even at the "runaway phase" of capital, about three-quarters of direct foreign investment went to other developed countries', and the numbers of women employed by TNCs in developing countries are a small proportion both of the female labour forces in those countries, and of the TNCs' total employment worldwide.[9]

On the other hand, multinational investment has had an impact that is greater than just the numbers involved:

- Much of the industrial production capacity in developing countries has been built up as part of the international production and market network[10] – the increase in export-oriented production, whether by local or foreign-owned companies, for example.

- Certain sectors and industries have been dominated by global production, most notably garments and electronics.

- The numbers of people, especially women, who work indirectly for foreign and global companies far exceeds those counted in the workforce.

- The concessions made by governments in terms of labour legislation and organization, and the fragmentation of work- places and workforces, have also had a significant negative impact on the development of trade unionism and the application of labour standards throughout the formal sectors of a number of countries.

WOMEN IN EXPORT INDUSTRIES □

Much early investment was in East and then Southeast Asia where highly polarized gender relations worked to the advantage of foreign investors. Women were traditionally excluded from most parts of the labour market in countries like Taiwan and Malaysia, so they had few points of comparison for wages and few contacts with trade unions. This lack of experience, the very young age of many of these women workers, allied with their socialization (perceived as 'docility'), and an ability to work neatly and well ('nimble fingers'), made them appear to be the ideal workforce. They are also a non-permanent workforce, since they are expected to leave the factory on marriage; indeed most of the contracts are on an insecure basis: temporary, casual, and often contingent on productivity quotas. An average 85 per cent of the workforce in export-oriented zones is female.

Among the first industries to move production to developing countries were textiles and clothing, traditional employers of

women. Food processing, plastics and pharmaceuticals followed, as did electronics; here, although the industry as a whole is capital-intensive, assembly work could be done more cheaply by hand, especially as the technology was changing so rapidly.[11]

More recently there has been a trend towards the 'globalization' of services, and indeed some 80 of the top 200 TNCs are service industries. The extent of relocation is not clear, and more research is needed in this area. Studies should incorporate a gender perspective, particularly in view of the many women in service industries. Cynthia Enloe gives this picture of a new type of factory: 'A hundred Barbadian women sit at a row of computer terminals. They enter 300,000 ticket reservations flowing from 2,000 daily flights of just a single US airline. In the same building one floor above them other women enter data from American medical insurance claims....'[12] Far from being separate from manufacturing, many services, especially those based on the collection and use of data, are essential to production processes. The service component of much manufacturing has increased, especially in the more technologically advanced industries and countries.

FREE TRADE ZONES □ Companies

looking to set up plants also needed a suitable infrastructure. Countries vied with each other to attract foreign investment, offering incentives including: tax advantages, subsidized utilities, and the opportunity to exploit natural resources. Free trade zones (FTZs) were created, also called export processing zones (EPZs), where companies could be exempted from national laws and regulations, including foreign exchange controls, restrictions on imports, taxation on profits and, especially, labour codes that established health and safety standards and gave workers the right to form unions and hold strikes.

The manual dexterity of the oriental female ...

The first substantial investment in special enclaves or zones was in Taiwan, Korea, Singapore and Hong Kong, followed by Southeast Asia. Japanese and US firms came in first, and then the European multinationals. About half the production was in electrical and electronic assembly.

Many US companies set up operations along the Mexican–US border, the so-called *maquiladora* area: 'The main policy of the Mexican government is getting dollars into the country. [To achieve this] it has broken the backbone of the unions and lowered working conditions. Ten years ago there were 80 *maquiladores* situated near the border with the US; now [1991] there are some 900 of these zones all over the country.... Young girls and women migrate to work there; they often earn the sole income for the whole family. This fact causes many difficulties between the men and the women in the family. [As investment increased] work processes changed. A division of labour has taken place with parts of the production process being transferred to the countryside, to isolated units and sometimes into the home.'[14]

Free trade zones have been called countries within countries because of the rules and conditions that apply in them, and because of their exemption from national legislation. They also have 'frontiers', that is to say, entry by non-authorized personnel is very difficult. Even where union activity is not expressly prohibited, the representatives of unions and other organizations find it difficult to get the necessary entry passes. In the Philippines, fences with armed guards surround export plants and zones.

WAGES AND CONDITIONS It has become a commonplace for the manage-ment of foreign-owned plants to claim that wages and conditions of work for 'their girls' are good, but in fact they are extremely variable and generally poor. In comparison with the company's country of origin, wages are likely to be in a ratio of between ten and twenty to one. In comparison with local wages, they are often below the official minimum wage, even if above what many people earn. They often depend on constantly increasing levels of productivity. Fluctuations in demand can result in enforced overtime at some times of the year and non-payment at others, especially for those working on a piece-rate basis.

Personnel policies often combine stringent discipline with the manipulation of the workers' leisure. Some plants control the women's lives twenty-four hours a day, by housing them in dormitory accommodation, and many structure recreational activities in such a way as to limit their freedom and encourage their loyalty to, and dependence on, the company. In *New Internationalist*, Rachael Grossman describes the beauty contests found in some Malaysian factories. These provide a break in the hard routine while encouraging the women to spend their earnings on Western-style cosmetics and clothes.[15]

Some of the factories appear to be clean and pleasant working environments, but health and safety hazards exist in all the industries. Garment workers are constantly exposed to dust and tiny fibres which cause chronic chest complaints and a range of allergies; a number of plastics used in other manufacturing processes also cause allergies. According to the US Occupational Health and Safety Administration, electronics is a high health-risk industry, exposing workers to dangerous chemicals and toxic fumes as well as causing migraine, eye strain and stress.[16] Sexual harassment is an additional hazard, as male managers and supervisors demand sexual

TOY FACTORY FIRE IN THAILAND

The price of a job can be a woman's life.... In May 1993 a dreadful fire burnt down a toy factory in Thailand, killing 240 people. Most of them were the women working in the factory, but the bodies of children were found too – children taken there by mothers who had no other way of looking after them. Workers had been aware of safety problems – indeed this was the third fire at the factory in the last few years – but had no union to negotiate for improvements. The factory produces toys, souvenirs and other plastic articles for export: 80 per cent go to the United States, 20 per cent to Europe. It is jointly owned by Hong Kong, Taiwanese, and Thai companies. A working group has been set up to offer support to victims and their families, to establish the causes of the fire, to put pressure on the company's management and the Thai government, and to organize an international campaign on health and safety standards in foreign-owned or export-oriented factories.

This is not the first time that a workplace tragedy has stimulated action to improve working conditions and strengthen the position of the workforce. A fire at the Triangle Waist factory in New York City in 1911 led to the first US laws on factory safety and to the formation of the International Ladies' Garment Workers' Union. The earthquake in Mexico City in 1985, revealing the dreadful conditions in hundreds of garment sweatshops, resulted in the creation of one of Mexico's few independent unions, the September 19 Union of Garment and Related Trades, which is mainly made up of and run by women.

favours from the women over whom they have almost unlimited control.

WHERE TO NOW? The free trade zones, once a distinct phenomenon with a clear place in certain international production processes, are now subject to a more complex combination of pressures and factors, though they are still growing fast. As competition increases, and recession hits harder, some companies have relocated to less developed, cheaper countries – first to the Philippines, Malaysia and Indonesia, then China, Sri Lanka and Bangladesh – where there are fewer and more recently established FTZs but where governments are anxious to 'catch up'. An increasing number of these companies are from the new rather than the old industrialized countries. The former socialist economies in Europe are offering similar arrangements in order to encourage investment.

Sixty countries now have zones of some sort; not all of them are physical enclaves, as some countries, among them Tunisia and Barbados, grant similar privileges to specified export companies that are wholly or partly foreign-owned.[17] In other countries, notably Brazil, the export orientation has been replaced by the production of goods for the domestic market. Employment levels are holding up because of the increasing number of zones or 'arrangements', but the structure of employment is changing, especially in the older zones. As the product mix changes, and technology develops, increasing use is being made of (usually male) technicians and other skilled workers.[18] Countries as diverse as Singapore and Mexico are seeing the female share of employment in FTZs declining.

THE QUESTION OF REGULATION The regulation of FTZs and TNCs remains an outstanding problem. It is unacceptable that any zone or enterprise should be outside the labour laws of the country where it is situated and, similarly, that it should flout international labour standards. The ILO has issued a Tripartite Declaration of Principles concerning multinational enterprises, and conducts regular surveys into its effect. The report from the fifth survey (1989–91) describes the efforts of some governments to bring the zones into line through legislation, and other initiatives to negotiate with the countries concerned.[19]

NGOs have been active in drawing attention to the social and economic conditions in certain FTZs; some work in or near the zones themselves and some act as research–pressure groups on TNC operations. The Women's International League for Peace and Freedom (WILPF) examined the problems of women workers in EPZs at an international seminar in 1990, and the following year a WILPF representative addressed the International Labour Conference, outlining the major hardships and abuses faced by women in many of the zones. She appealed for the ILO to help countries to develop and implement national regulations, and proposed co-operation between the ILO and WILPF. This is an example of a particularly effective form of alliance, combining the local knowledge and experience of activists with the international weight and legislative role of an inter-governmental organization.

THE ELECTRONICS INDUSTRY □

Microelectronics was the vanguard industry in the new FTZs of the 1960s and 1970s; by 1971 all major US manufacturers in the field had overseas operations. The industry lends itself well to fragmented manufacturing and assembly because the components are small and light in relation to their value.

Microelectronics is still the predominant light industry, and has spread far beyond the FTZs. '[It] is not only the largest and fastest growing manufacturing industry in the world today, but also the most globally diversified in the location of its production facilities.... Women on opposite sides of the world work under strikingly similar conditions, assembling the same products, sometimes even for the same transnationals.'[20] While the first major relocation in electronics was from industrialized to developing countries, the second has been from the factory into the sweatshop or home. Even in rural areas, increasing numbers of women are involved in electronic outworking.

I test around 3,500 chips a day. I work in the optical test section where I look through a microscope to test the chips before they are bonded. After the training period they set my quota at 15 trays a day. Now I have to test 25 trays a day. There are between 160 and 180 chips in each tray. My shift starts at six and goes on until two in the afternoon. They don't let us talk during work but we can talk during our breaks. We have a ten-minute break at eight and a fifteen-minute lunch break at 9.15.

After six months I became sick with red-eye [conjunctivitis]. Other friends at work got sick too, and my family caught it. I like to buy my brothers and sisters noodle soup but if I buy it for all of us it costs a whole day's salary.[21]

TEXTILES AND GARMENTS □

Textiles have played a key role in international trade for thousands of years, and were central to the industrial revolution in Europe in the nineteenth century. Today, with clothing, they have an equally important role in the economies of many developing countries. The textile and garment sector provided the initial stage of the industrialization process in many countries, and was also instrumental in the transition from import substitution to export promotion. The two industries (production of cloth and the processing of it into garments) account for over one-quarter of

The subcontracting chain can be very long: home knitters in Peru

all manufactured exports from developing countries.[22]

The textile industry has seen rapid technological change over the past two decades. New methods have cut by 40 per cent the number of workers needed to produce the same amount of cloth. At the same time, production has become concentrated into the hands of only a few TNCs. Although some of the NIEs, and China, have made inroads into world trade, ten out of the fifteen top exporters are among the old industrialized countries.[23]

The garment industry is highly fragmented, and in many cases the production or assembly of garments has now become completely separated from their retailing. Most export garment factories are not subsidiaries of TNCs but independent suppliers who carry the risks of a business but have no control over most of its operations. They are heavily dependent on 'the buyer', and also on changes in fashions and new clauses in trade agreements. On the other hand, the low start-up costs in the clothing sector, and its labour-intensive nature, have made it an important vehicle for industrial development in some of the poorest countries, such as Bangladesh. Only the largest firms are able to invest in new technology, and at present there is no viable alternative to the machinist for most functions. Some four-fifths of the work on each garment can be contracted out. The sub-contracting chain may stretch halfway across the world.

TECHNOLOGICAL CHANGE □ A key element of industrialization from its earliest phase has been the introduction of mechanization, first to perform productive tasks and then, as it became more sophisticated, to organize the processes of production, including the workforce. The globalization

THE GARMENT INDUSTRY IN BANGLADESH ...

Bangladesh, one of the poorest countries in the world, is an overwhelmingly agricultural economy where many people are dependent on low-paid casual labour – but there isn't enough to go round. For many years its main export earner was jute, but this was badly hit by the general decline in commodity prices and the growing use of plastic packaging.

Bangladesh saw no industrial growth in the course of the 1980s, except in the export garment sector. Between 1986 and 1992 the number of garment factories increased from 177 to 1,100. The value of exports rose from two million dollars in 1980 to just under one billion in 1991-92. Some half-million new jobs have been created, 85 per cent of them held by women. Most of the garment factories are not owned by TNCs, although foreign capital is invested in some of them. The factories, however, all produce for the big Western retailers. Hourly wages in Bangladesh are the lowest among garment workers in Asia. Minimum wage, working hours, sick pay, and health and safety regulations are ignored by most employers. The women work behind locked gates and are body-searched as they leave. The average age of workers is seventeen, though a number start at eleven or twelve. Many women hide the fact that they are married and have children.

Farida Akhter is the director of UBINIG, an action–research group: 'Despite the appalling conditions we come across every day, I am hopeful that women garment workers can win improvements.... Some problems – like the violence against women workers – have started to get a little better.... Of course, lifting quotas on shirts from Bangladesh won't automatically help workers, but it will certainly strengthen their bargaining position.'

Ben Jackson, *Threadbare: How the Rich Stitch up the World's Rag Trade*, World Development Movement, London, 1992

... AND IN THE NETHERLANDS: THE STORY OF A BLOUSE

'Company X subcontracts both in the Third World and in the Netherlands; we look here at the subcontracting chain of X in the Netherlands, and how a blouse might be produced.

The X buyer contacts a middleman and asks for a new type of blouse, a nice blouse for Sundays and holidays. The middleman buys a design, the buyer changes a few details and then accepts it. He orders 10,000 blouses for delivery the next week. The middleman buys a large quantity of cloth, and sends it to a specialist cutter, then he subcontracts the making-up of the blouses to a small firm. An average sweatshop produces about 2,000 blouses a week so the middleman subcontracts to 5 different firms. The low price they charge may depend on their being illegal or semi-legal, with poor pay and working conditions. Quite often the sweatshops subcontract part of the production to homeworkers. The blouses return to the sweatshop to be finished and have the X label sewn on. The middleman then sells the blouses to X, and X sells the blouses to ... you?'

SOMO, *Subcontracting Practices in the Netherlands and in the Third World*

of investment and the new flexibility – in labour, production, and marketing – were both made possible by developments in technology, especially data processing and telecommunications.

The advances in technology reinforced

existing trends in management towards the division of jobs into separate tasks performed by different units. Thus, technology may promote not only a polarization of the workforce between skilled and unskilled workers but a general fragmentation, taking workers away from the benefits and protection of unions and collective bargaining. More recently, high technology has been the instrument that makes it possible for companies to respond almost instantly to changing demand. One example is the fashion firm Benetton, whose shops across the world are directly linked from the cash register to a computer at the head office in Italy. This means they know immediately what is selling, and when stock needs replacing; orders are dispatched from a giant warehouse operated by one controller, a few robots and nineteen maintenance staff.[24]

HEALTH AND SAFETY HAZARDS New technology has caused new health and safety problems. The electronics industry, claimed by the Federation of Hong Kong Industries to be 'the most technologically advanced, safe and clean industry in the world', gives workers health problems from eye strain and myopia to backache, bronchitis, stomach disorders and stress. Personal computers, one of the most widely used of technological innovations, can cause so many different types of strain that guidelines for their safe use have been issued by industrial health authorities and trade unions. Measures need to be taken to guard against glare, bad positioning of the arms, spine and legs of the user, and against long periods of use without a break. Different rays and chemicals are also among the hazards of the new technology, and the ILO collaborates with the WHO to set guidelines for occupational health and safety. Convention No. 170 and Recommendation No. 177, on safety in the use of chemicals at work, were adopted by

the International Labour Conference in 1990.

THE IMPACT ON JOBS There is a danger of oversimplifying the effects of technology, and overlooking, for example, its use in improving working conditions and minimizing the physical differences between men and women in production. Technology is a tool of entrepreneurs and policymakers and, depending on their priorities (and the vigilance of workers and their organizations) may conceivably bring social as well as economic benefits. The most common application of technology, however, appears to be geared to increasing productivity – so much so that some commentators now speak of the 'uncoupling' of production from employment.[25]

Are men and women affected equally by the mechanization, or automation, of different industrial processes? To some extent it depends. Where technology has changed work processes so that a job based on strength and/or skill has become lighter and supposedly less skilled as a result of technological change, it tends to go to women. Its status is downgraded, and women can be paid less. One example is the printing industry, formerly dominated by men who had served long apprenticeships, now within the reach of anyone who can type.

But, as Hilary Standing points out, technology can also lead to the masculinization of what were formerly women's jobs, 'when, for instance, the men assert a stronger claim to what employment is left after rationalization, or when the technological "upgrading" of jobs causes men to be regarded as more suitable'.[26] She shows how, in the Indian jute industry, a female workforce of 45,000 in 1921 was down to 7,000 in 1972. First, a number of the tasks performed by the women were mechanized, but second – and in spite of previously rigid job boundaries along gender

PHOTO: IIO/J. MAILLARD

Women must not be excluded from the benefits of new technology

lines – most of the remaining 'women's tasks' were taken over by men as unemployment rose, and it was accepted by management and unions that men had the greater 'right' to them.

It is also becoming clear that technological developments have resulted in a fall in the proportion of unskilled workers to total industrial employment. As women are generally overrepresented among unskilled workers, they have been proportionately more affected. Where employment opportunities are still expanding, they are often in high-tech, high-skill areas where women are underrepresented, and very proactive training and employment promotion packages will be necessary if female workers are not to be further excluded.

THE ROLE OF TRADE ☐ Industrial development takes place within the con-text of world trade, which affects what is produced, how and where. A basic condition of structural adjustment programmes is fuller participation in the world trading system, both as importers and exporters. And even the most self-reliant countries need some foreign exchange for necessary imports. As a farmer in Chad replied, when asked why he didn't just grow food instead of cotton at rock-bottom prices: 'You can't pay the doctor in millet.'[27]

As the principal markets for developing countries are the industrialized countries, it would seem logical, as well as fair, for them to promote production, industrial development, and exports in the poor countries by opening their markets and paying fair prices. What actually happens is that the rich countries set tariffs and quotas on imports, especially of manufactured goods, as well as paying low prices

TARIFFS are duties on imports, which generally increase as more value is added to the product by processing. For example: the EC tariff is 3 per cent on cocoa beans, but 16 per cent on chocolate.

QUOTAS limit the quantity of goods that may be imported. They are directed towards processed goods rather than primary commodities, and most are imposed by rich countries to 'protect' their industries from competition from the poor countries.

for the raw materials on which the developing countries depend.

The developing countries – as colonies and since – have been encouraged to produce a narrow range of commodities for the industrialized countries to process and consume. Many commodities are at their lowest price levels since the 1930s, while the cost of these countries' imports from rich countries – the spare parts, fertilizer, and medicines they need – keeps going up. This is the trade trap: poor countries are earning less for the same amount exported, and paying more for the same amount imported. In 1972, 50 tonnes of cotton could buy eight trucks – but it could not purchase even two in 1987.[28]

DISINCENTIVES TO INDUSTRIALIZATION

One solution to the problem of dependence on one, or a very few, primary commodities is diversification, especially into the processing of raw materials or into appropriate manufacturing. This would make countries less vulnerable and help the expansion of the industrial sector. Many Western experts advise this course, and technical assistance is given to strengthen export industries. At the same time, Western governments devise complex conditions and agreements to protect their own industrial development and to block that of their weaker trading partners.

One protective mechanism with a direct

impact on the lives of many women is the Multi-Fibre Arrangement (MFA), which sets complex rules for trade in textiles and clothing. Within a broad framework, each importing country sets annual quotas on each exporter's products. The importers in the current arrangement are nine industrialized countries or blocs, most notably the EC and the USA; the thirty-two exporters listed include all Third World countries with any significant clothing or textile exports, and four central and east European countries. MFA experts Irene Trela and John Whalley at UNCTAD calculated that at 1986 prices the MFA alone cost the Third World some $26 billion a year; but in terms of distorted trade, blocked development, and lost employment opportunities the cost is incalculable.[29]

The major trading nations and international financial institutions all promote the principle of free trade. The main objective of the General Agreement on Tariffs and Trade (GATT), for example, although originally envisaged as an organization with wider powers to promote and regulate world trade, is to eliminate barriers to trade. Set up by twenty-three major trading nations in 1947, GATT was designed to expand world trade by reducing tariffs and other protectionist measures. It has certainly stimulated trade, and has succeeded in lowering a number of tariffs over the years, but mainly between the rich countries who dominate negotiations. Its terms have been changed in seven 'rounds' of negotiations, the most recent being the Uruguay Round. In spite of the fact that the MFA breaks both the free trade spirit of GATT, and several of its basic rules, the arrangement is renegotiated every few years in the GATT Textile Committee.

The United Nations Conference on Trade and Development (UNCTAD) was set up in 1964, at the prompting of less developed countries aware of their disadvantage in international economic relations. The objective was to counterbalance the domination of the rich countries in other spheres (for example, GATT and other special agreements) but its powers are few. It does not contribute to the development of international policies on trade and is more or less limited to providing advice, information and technical assis-

tance to developing countries. It did, however, succeed in negotiating a General System of Preferences which grants preferential treatment to certain products from developing countries.

WHAT CAN WE DO? Trade unions and NGOs in the North and the South are urging the inclusion of 'social clauses' in trade agreements. These would establish the rights of workers and in some cases

WHAT GATT SHOULD KNOW ABOUT WOMEN – AND WHAT WOMEN SHOULD KNOW ABOUT GATT

Although there is a substantial literature on the impact of industrialization (especially global production) on women in different parts of the world, many of the connections between women and the macroeconomy remain to be made. There is a dearth of research on the impact of GATT and other trade agreements on women. And yet adjustments to the MFA, for example, could have a greater impact on women, for good or ill, than one hundred income-generating projects.

Trade is not simply an economic mechanism; it depends on the production and consumption of individuals, as well as a number of structural factors. Trade agreements – multilateral and bilateral, formal and informal – need to be analysed with reference to their social impact, including a gender-specific evaluation. What would a gender analysis add? This is not simply an academic exercise to assess the 'impact on women'. An export orientation has consequences for production processes, perhaps encouraging more flexibility and/or the introduction of new technology. As outlined above, these will not affect men and women in the same way. The labour market has different uses for male and female workers; similarly the availability of

women workers is on different terms and conditions from men's, and impacts on households and communities in different ways. To understand the full impact of a decision to extend the land area available for cattle-raising, to grow more pineapples for Del Monte, or to mechanize spinning – any of which decisions might result from new or changed trade agreements – it is necessary to understand the effect of the decision on men and on women, and on women in both their reproductive and productive roles. Conversely, it is also necessary to understand how women's unpaid and underpaid work impacts on trade and production.

Questions should be asked by concerned activists and by development planners. They are also the responsibility of those who invest in and those who regulate trade. Much work is required in order to turn the questions into policies and strategies for trade and investment. More comparative studies are also needed on the effects on women of free market strategies versus state intervention, and of different forms of state intervention. These enquiries need to be complemented by research to establish how the proper use of women's labour contributes to economic and social development.

promote certain social or environmental objectives. A related idea is the 'tying' of aid or investment to programmes that demonstrably integrate women, for example. There is a strong case for a new international trading organization to be set up to carry out a range of standard-setting and regulatory functions such as these. Pressure is mounting for the creation of a body based on one member – one vote, transparent decision-making procedures, and the power to curb the current dominance of the United States, the EC and Japan. At the same time, the position of the poorer trading nations would be greatly strengthened if South–South trade and exchange were increased. A number of attempts have been made in the past, but perhaps the time is ripe for women – with their extensive trading experience and commitment to network and alliance building – to give a new lead.

NGOs have done excellent work in research and lobbying on trade issues; it cannot be covered comprehensively here, but some of the principal approaches include:

- GATT monitoring, and the development of alternative trading proposals;

- TNC monitoring, and lobbying for the application of standards;

- research and campaigning on particular sectors or countries, focusing public attention on conditions of workers and terms of trade.

An important strategy in all cases has been international contact and exchange – between workers in the same industry, for example, and activists with the same concerns and goals. Because trade is part of the wider economic scene, it has been crucial to make connections with other issues, such as debt and structural adjustment. An initiative of particular interest to women is the Women's Alternative Economic Summit, which provides a forum for activists and researchers working towards economic justice for women.

CONSUMER ACTION International investment and trade not only provide a link between workers, they also connect producers and consumers. Action by concerned consumers – 'the power of the purse' – is gaining importance as a way of putting pressure on businesses. An education package on the garment industry, produced by Women Working Worldwide, was a major factor in persuading a large UK chain store, Littlewoods, to adopt a code of practice for its garment suppliers. This seems to be the first time a major retailer has issued such a code of practice, and it represents a crucial step towards ensuring decent and fair working conditions for garment workers internationally. The Dutch group SOMO (Centre for Research on Multinational Corporations), whose study of garment subcontracting is cited above, has launched the 'Clean Clothes Campaign' to raise public awareness and get the big manufacturer-retailers to take responsibility for their workers all along the subcontracting chain.

NGOs in a number of industrialized countries have set up alternative trading organizations. These arrange the import of goods from developing countries on fair terms; usually a price is paid slightly above the market rate and it goes directly to poor producers not agents. The original outlets were often Third World shops, but some products are now on the shelves of major supermarkets, with a message about fair trade on each packet. A more ambitious initiative along this line is the Fairtrade Mark. Manufacturers can apply to an independent foundation, set up by a group of development NGOs in the UK, for the right to use the Fairtrade Mark – this guar-

antees that the producers have been paid a fair price, and work in safe and decent conditions.

CONCLUSION ☐ Many questions have been raised about the costs of attracting international investment and the relatively low benefits gained. But what about the new female workforce, brought into the market economy in such numbers? Haven't they gained anything? This is a vital question because one strategy in the face of the subordination of women is to encourage their participation in the labour force.

It is undeniable that many new jobs for women are low-paid and insecure, and give them few transferable skills. If paid work simply exposes women to new forms of exploitation outside the home as well as within it, and to an increased workload, they may be worse off than before. An ILO report on employment promotion in Indonesia speaks of the demand for female labour 'being predicated on the implicit elasticity of their labour supply and an explicit inferiority of treatment'.[30]

On the other hand, there may be new opportunities. 'With industrialization, women in the Asian NICs [newly industrialized countries] have for the first time in history been able to get paid work instead of playing the centuries-old women's role of unpaid mother–wife–labourer....'[31]

Although evidence is mixed as to the changed status of women within the family when they start earning a wage, a woman's status is enhanced in her own eyes. The workplace also gives women the chance to

Guarantees a **better deal** for Third World Producers — Fairtrade

meet, socialize and organize. The OECD calls the current phase of industrialization 'a dynamic process [which] offers a real opportunity to dismantle current gender-based occupational segregation'.[32] Another positive factor is the growing understanding of the dynamics of industrial and economic development: this is leading planners and entrepreneurs to give new priority to the development of human resources.

These trends are not in themselves indicators of progress on women's rights, but they represent possibilities. In order to turn them into fact, more is needed:

... it would seem to be of paramount importance to identify in advance those growth branches and emerging technologies in which women can in the future play a greater role than in most industries in the past, and to formulate ... skill requirements. It appears reasonable to assume that at a time when traditional production processes are transformed by technological change the opportunities to overcome gender-based occupational classifications are comparatively great, due to the lower strength of vested interests.[33]

1. United Nations Industrial Development Organization (UNIDO), *Women and Human Resource Development for Industry*, UNIDO, Vienna, 1988, p. 8.
2. Ruth Pearson, 'Gender issues in industrialization', in Tom Hewitt, Hazel Johnson, and David Wield (eds), *Industrialization and Development*, Oxford University Press, Oxford, 1992.
3. UNIDO.
4. Swasti Mitter, *Common Fate, Common Bond: Women in the Global Economy*, Pluto Press, London, 1986, p. 25.
5. Hilary Standing, 'Employment', in Lise Østergaard (ed.), *Gender and Development: a Practical Guide*, Routledge, London, 1992.
6. Anneke van Luijken and Swasti Mitter, *Unseen Phenomenon: the Rise in Homeworking*, Change, London, n.d., p. 4.
7. See Swasti Mitter and Ruth Pearson, *Global Information Processing: the Emergence of Software Services and Data Entry Jobs in Selected Developing Countries*, ILO, Geneva, 1992.
8. UNIDO, p. 11.
9. Valentine Moghadam, *Gender, Development and Policy: Toward Equity and Empowerment*, United Nations University, World Institute for Development Economics Research, Helsinki, 1990, p. 16.
10. UNIDO, p. 7.
11. UNIDO.
12. Cynthia Enloe, 'Silicon tricks and the two dollar woman', in *New Internationalist*, No. 227, 1992.
13. Mitter, p. 45.
14. Itziar Lozano, 'Mexico into the world economy', in *News from IRENE*, No. 15–16, 1992, pp. 27–8.
15. Rachael Grossman, 'Miss Micro', in *New Internationalist*, No. 150, 1985.
16. Rosalinda Pinedo-Ofreneo, 'Issues in the Philippine electronics industry', in *News from IRENE*, No. 7, 1988.
17. Ana T. Romero, 'Export processing zones: insights from a recent ILO survey', in *Labour Education*, 2/91, 1993.
18. See, for example, Sally Baden and Susan Joekes, 'Gender issues in the development of the special economic zones and open areas in the People's Republic of China', paper for a seminar on women's participation in economic development held at Fudan University, Shanghai, April 1993 (Institute of Development Studies, University of Sussex, 1993).
19. Romero.
20. Geraldine Reardon, *Common Interests: Women Organising in Global Electronics*, Women Working Worldwide, London, 1991.
21. Grossman.
22. Ben Jackson, *Threadbare: How the Rich Stitch up the World's Rag Trade*, World Development Movement, London, 1992.
23. Ibid.
24. Ibid.
25. UNIDO.
26. Standing, p. 65.
27. Belinda Coote, *The Trade Trap: Poverty and the Global Commodity Markets*, Oxfam, Oxford, 1992.
28. World Development Movement briefing paper on trade (forthcoming).
29. Jackson
30. ILO/UNDP, *A Comprehensive Women's Employment Strategy for Indonesia*, ILO Regional Office for Asia and the Pacific, Bangkok, 1993.
31. Trini Leung, 'Women workers in newly industrialised countries of Asia: problems and issues', in ISIS/CAW, *Industrial Women Workers in Asia*, ISIS International Women's Journal, No. 4, 1985.
32. Organisation for Economic Cooperation and Development (OECD), *Structural Change: the Role of Women*, OECD, Paris, 1991, pp. 14–15.
33. UNIDO.

6 THE STRUCTURES OF LEARNING: BARRIER OR KEY TO THE DOOR?

Without education you are nothing in this world. I wish that I could be born again. I wouldn't get married so young, and I would learn and learn until I died.

WOMAN FARMER IN ZIMBABWE[1]

THE WAY EDUCATION IS ORGANIZED and delivered depends on the attitudes and priorities of societies and their decision-makers – but education also helps to form those attitudes and priorities. There is an implicit tension at all levels of the education system between its potential to promote social change and its role as defender of prevailing norms and values. This extends to the response of education to the labour market: to what extent should it help to supply the skills that the market identifies as necessary, and to what it extent does it attempt to shape the market to make it more efficient and more egalitarian?

THE GLOBAL PICTURE □ Education and training for girls and women have long been seen as key measures to improve women's social and economic status. Encouragement should be drawn from some of the figures on school attendance. The enrolment of girls in primary and secondary education has caught up with that of boys in most developed countries and in Latin America and the Caribbean, and nearly equals it in East and Southeast Asia and in the Pacific region. It is increasing faster than that of boys in sub-Saharan Africa and South Asia but from a lower starting point; South Asia is the only area where girls' secondary enrolments are less than half those of boys.[2]

The extension of primary education has boosted literacy. Between 1970 and 1990 literacy rates improved significantly, especially among younger women: the numbers of illiterate women aged between twenty and twenty-four decreased from 80 to 50 per cent in sub-Saharan Africa, for example, and from nearly 80 per cent to just over 40 per cent in northern Africa and western Asia.[3] The gap between men and women has remained wide in every region, however, and population growth means that the actual number of illiterate girls and women has increased. Rates are very much higher in rural than in urban areas, even among young women. A World Bank study found that 80 per cent of rural women workers in India were illiterate.[4]

The participation of young women in further and higher education has increased, in overall numbers and in some traditionally male-dominated areas too – though the evidence is not entirely consistent. In over thirty countries more women are in higher education than men, but regional differences are great. There are fewer than 30 female per 100 male students in sub-Saharan Africa and southern Asian countries. In all regions except Africa women make up at least 30 per cent of science and engineering students. For law and business the numbers are more or less equal in the developed regions and Latin America, approaching 40 per cent women in Asia and the Pacific, and 26 per cent in Africa.[5]

Education is mainly considered here in relation to women's employment opportunities and social status. It is nevertheless worth noting that higher levels of education among women are also associated with later marriage and child-bearing, smaller families, and a higher standard of health and nutrition.

Table 6.1: PERCENTAGE OF FEMALE SCHOOL ENROLMENTS, 1975—90

CONTINENTS, MAJOR AREAS AND GROUPS OF COUNTRIES		Percentage female enrolment by level		
		1st level	2nd level	3rd level
World Total	1975	45	43	41
	1990	46	44	45
Africa	1975	42	35	26
	1990	45	42	30
America	1975	49	49	44
	1990	49	50	52
Asia	1975	43	38	30
	1990	45	41	35
Europe (including former USSR)	1975	49	49	45
	1990	49	50	49
Oceania	1975	47	48	40
	1990	48	49	51
Developed countries	1975	49	49	44
	1990	49	50	50
Developing countries	1975	44	38	33
	1990	45	42	37

SOURCE: UNESCO STATISTICAL YEARBOOK 1992.

THE CONTEXT OF EDUCATION ☐ Education is not, of course, only a question of institutions; a broad range of forces influence the development of individuals, their educational experience, and their later working life. The same political priorities and cultural values that affect employment also shape education. The availability and quality of schools and teachers depend on resources and on political choices. In some regions schools are not universally available, especially in the rural areas, and in others fees are charged. Cuts in public spending on education have resulted in school closures and reduced opportunities for girls and women. Attendance is also influenced by local attitudes to the value of education and by the limits on girls' mobility.

Boys and girls do not arrive at school on an equal footing; gender affects both their access to schooling and their experience at school. It also shapes girls' expectations of what school can offer them, and of what they themselves can achieve. The process starts long before they get to school: in many societies the birth of a girl is tolerated rather than celebrated. In others it is actively regretted. Female infanticide is not a thing of the past, and in some countries it contributes to an imbalance in the ratio of men to women. In spite of women's longer life expectancy, slightly under half of the world's population is female, and in a number of countries (almost all of them in Asia) there are fewer than 95 women to 100 men. Although girl children almost invariably work harder than boys, they are more likely to be undernourished. In a significant number of countries in Asia, Africa and Latin America, mortality rates for chil-

Table 6.2: ILLITERACY LEVELS AMONG YOUNG WOMEN

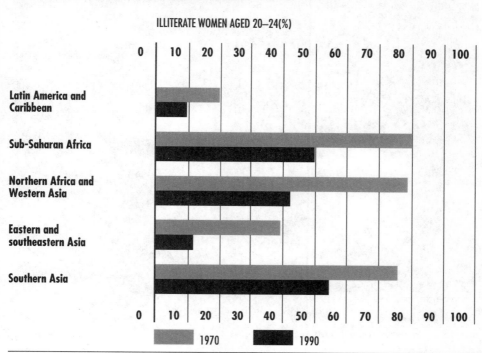

ILLITERATE WOMEN AGED 20–24(%)

1970   1990

SOURCE: UNITED NATIONS (The World's Women: Trends and Statistics, 1970–1990, United Nations, New York, 1991.)

dren under five years old are higher among girls than boys.[6]

Many parents' expectations are different for their sons than for their daughters. A girl's future is more often seen in terms of marriage than a job. In many societies, when, whom and on what terms a girl marries are the most important considerations, and determine her role and status. Even where it is quite common for girls to think in terms of a 'career', most also realize that some form of compromise will be necessary between this and their reproductive role: a compromise few men anticipate or make.

Children in Britain often count out the discarded stones of fruit such as cherries by chanting 'tinker, tailor, soldier, sailor, rich man, poor man, beggar man, thief' – one word to each stone. For boys, the final word denotes what they will be; for girls, it denotes the person they will marry.

Although girls are increasingly likely to get some schooling, in poorer countries it may well be interrupted because they are needed to help at home, or to bring in an income. It may also stop earlier than for a boy: adolescent marriage and pregnancy are still very common in some regions, making higher education, even the completion of secondary schooling, impossible for many girls. A study for the United Nations Division for the Advancement of Women (DAW) suggests that in countries badly affected by debt and recession, girls are being taken out of school at a faster rate than boys.[7]

THE EDUCATIONAL EXPERIENCE □

Ensuring that education has a positive impact on the status and role of women is more than just a matter of

89

PHOTO: ILO

More girls in education: a science class in Sri Lanka

checking enrolment rates. While the numbers are important, and parity must be a target, we should also question the content, methodology and structures of learning. To assess the impact of education, and plan for future needs, means taking into account both its quantitative and qualitative aspects.

Education has the potential to challenge stereotypes about male and female roles, to offer alternative ideas, and to equip young women to pursue a range of possibilities. But because gender impacts on education as on other social systems, school is more likely to echo and reinforce prevailing attitudes. Some subjects are seen as more appropriate or useful for girls, and others for boys. Girls rarely receive positive encouragement to try the technical and scientific subjects for which boys are supposed to have a natural aptitude; they are not

shown the practical application of these subjects to a wide range of occupations, as well as outside the work environment. Girls and boys are often treated differently too; in a mixed class teachers are found to spend more time putting questions to, and answering the questions of,

WHO SAYS BOYS ARE BETTER AT MATHS?

'It is time to put to rest one of the most widespread of all myths about the sexes. Men are not better at mathematics than women. This is not to say that men and women have identical patterns of achievement at maths. It may also be that they have different attitudes about its relevance. But the notion of some kind of inherent male advantage when it comes to numbers ... is flatly contradicted by the evidence. "The difference in maths ability between men and women is so close to zero ... that we should consider it zero," says Janet Hyde, a psychologist at the University of Wisconsin who recently completed a massive comparative analysis of maths performance and gender.'[8]

boys. Gender differences are reinforced by several factors: the lack of role models for girls in materials and among staff; inadequate equipment in girls' schools; poor career guidance; and a lack of motivation or inexperience on the part of staff in promoting equal opportunities.

It is important to recognize that many schemes and programmes have been devised with the aim of changing structures and attitudes to give girls more encouragement, especially in the secondary schools of some industrialized nations. These have generally been initiated by ministries of education, local authorities and/or national women's bureaux, but do not yet seem to have resulted in significant changes in the subject and career choices of boys and girls. It is clearly not enough simply to 'encourage' girls to make different choices; pedagogical methods must be improved, as must the training and employment opportunities that girls can see before them.[9]

FURTHER EDUCATION AND VOCATIONAL TRAINING □ Despite impressive increases in the numbers of women at higher levels of the education system, there is a persistent concentration of women in traditionally 'female' courses, especially in vocational training. Between 1975 and 1990 the percentage of women in engineering in India rose from 1 to 10 per cent. In a few colleges they represent 30 per cent of students, but their numbers remain low in the more prestigious institutes.[11] In Sri Lanka, in 1987 all the students on industrial and regular sewing courses were women, while in electrical work, construction, carpentry, metalwork, and agriculture all were men.[12]

Enrolments for 1991 at the Academy, Namibia's main institution for further and higher education, show women outnumbering men by more than two to one, but a significant gender imbalance persists in many subjects. Women are underrepresented in science, economics, management and, in particular, agriculture. They predominate in fields of study such as health sciences and education, which prepare them for stereotypical careers in nursing and teaching.[13]

EQUAL EDUCATION IN DENMARK
The Equal Status Council in Denmark has developed the following recommendations to influence educational policy:

- Schools should motivate children in such a way that girls and boys determine their interests, educational and occupational choices, and adult role without reference to the roles traditionally reserved for the two sexes.

- Guidelines must be prepared on the organization of teaching and the adaptation of curricula so that school activities, from primary level onwards, are based on the principle of equal merit and opportunities.

- Preparatory work for scientific and technical subjects should be started well before puberty, when attitudes and prejudices become more fixed.

- Concern for others, caring skills and an understanding of human rights should be fostered through all school activities. Life skills should be taught, and participatory and co-operative work should be encouraged.

- Education must develop the self-confidence and sense of personal value of girls, in particular. The benefits of limited periods of single-sex education should be investigated. Materials should be reviewed for gender stereotyping, and positive examples and messages should be incorporated into texts and teaching aids.

- Technical and scientific subjects should be taught in a social context with reference to 'real life' experience. Subjects should be grouped in such a way that choices do not have to be made between arts and sciences.

- Schools should be open to the world of work, the family, and leisure and community activities. Adult life should be presented as a whole, and both paid and unpaid work should be considered and appreciated. The broadest possible range of role models should be presented.[10]

It is particularly remarkable that women's participation in advanced agricultural studies is so low, often around 20 per cent, especially in those countries where agricultural activities predominate and women are the backbone of the agricultural labour force.

The number of women training for 'male' jobs in West Germany rose from 2.5 to 8.4 per cent between 1977 and 1987. But even in 1987 31 per cent of women were trained for only four occupations: hairdresser, shop assistant, secretary, and medical assistant; 70 per cent of all women in vocational training were concentrated in the fifteen occupations most frequently chosen by women.[14] Studies from the USA show a similar imbalance: women predominate in health, home economics, and office and business programmes; men predominate in technical preparation, manual trades, and agriculture. Additionally, it is interesting to note the places where women and men are trained: for the female-dominated occupations the classroom is predominant, while enterprise-based courses and apprenticeships are generally the training ground for male-dominated technical jobs.[15]

Women are less likely to receive workplace training because of the nature of their employment in dead-end jobs, their non-standard contracts, and their overrepresentation in small enterprises without training facilities or resources. Managers and professional staff receive more training than manual workers, which also weights the training balance against women. Gender bias can be quite subtle: in the British youth training schemes of the 1980s half the young women were in positions labelled simply 'office', 'clerical', or 'clerk-typist' while eleven out of twelve male clerical trainees were receiving more specific training or labelling, for example, insurance clerk, salaries clerk and so on.[16]

EDUCATION, TRAINING AND EMPLOYMENT ☐ Poor co-ordination between school and vocational training, as well as between training and employment needs, is a widespread problem. This leads to a waste of human potential and undermines social and economic development. Many girls and women remain outside any training systems while funds are invested in training women for jobs for which there is no demand or for ghetto occupations. The numbers of women in technical and vocational training in areas of priority for development plans are particularly low. While millions of women are unable to find income-earning opportunities for lack of qualifications, there is a desperate need for skilled personnel in many countries. In spite of experiments in some countries, changes in education and training over recent years appear to have been fewer and of a more superficial nature than the radical restructuring of many aspects of employment. The OECD reports a growing mismatch between skills and jobs in both industrialized and developing countries. It points to a need for upgraded technical skills, for greater versatility, and for the development of non-technical 'human capabilities', such as creativity, communication, and co-operation.[17]

The impact of education on women's employment to date is not easy to assess. In the developed regions, where the numbers of girls in school are equal to those of boys, there has also been a substantial increase in the numbers of women in the labour force. The issue, however, is not just one of access to education and training but of equality of outcomes. Women's employment, as discussed in Chapter 2, is concentrated in a narrow range of occupations and at the lower levels of pay and responsibility. A vicious circle exists whereby gender bias results in asymmetrical educational opportunities; these contribute to job segregation, which in turn reinforces the sexual division of labour and gender inequality. Where and how can this vicious circle be broken?

AN INTEGRATED STRATEGY Fundamental changes of attitude are necessary before women can make progress in education, training and employment; at the same time, action in the field of education and training can help bring about these changes. Gretchen Goodale, ILO specialist in women's training, argues that for vocational education and training to lead to greater equality in the labour market, a multi-level, integrated approach is necessary. On the one hand this entails addressing the constraints on girls' and women's access to and performance in training: such areas as the streaming of students, gender bias in learning materials, trainers' attitudes, and vocational counselling and placement services. On the other hand it means recognizing the broader social, economic and political context of education and training, in particular the issue of the roles women are being trained to perform.[18] Key partners need to be identified, from parents to policy-makers. Methods used might include public information through the mass media, support services for trainees, and financial incentives for employers. The systems and institutions of vocational educational and training themselves need to do the following:

- link backwards with primary and secondary education;

- link forwards with employers and trade unions;

- lobby governments for legal and policy changes;

- change their own structures (from staff and student recruitment to course content).[19]

A USEFUL REPORT
Some 100 VET (vocational education and training) institutions in the Commonwealth Association of Polytechnics in Africa (CAPA) have co-operated in order to increase the numbers of women among their staffs and students, with the long-term objective of enhancing women's role in technical education and employment. First, research was carried out in a sample of institutions (twenty polytechnics in nine countries), and with key groups affecting the total environment of vocational training. The project also reviewed successful initiatives taken by other agencies, and then worked out detailed plans to achieve equity goals, involving policy and procedural changes in all areas, as well as public information campaigns. Essential elements of success were judged to be the commitment of directors, an adequate allocation of resources, and systematic monitoring. The report produced – entitled *Women in Technical Trades* – contains the research findings and recommendations for action, plus a useful checklist for monitoring female participation.[20]

UNIDO emphasizes the fact that training is just one part of human resource planning and development.

Educational and training policies need to be an integral part of a country's social and economic system and in particular will have to respond to its overall economic strategies and policies, and the major internal and external trends affecting them. In this context, dynamic human resource planning acquires special significance.[21]

As the Asian Regional Office of the ILO concluded in relation to Indonesia:

The challenge is to raise awareness of the significance of the links between training, productivity, profits and long-term competitiveness, and to work out the respective responsibilities for the provision of training (by the Government, employers, and public and private training institutions) and for ensuring equality of access to such training.[22]

Many countries, especially in Africa, are

93

Responding to women's different needs: basic medical course in Fiji

facing increasing problems of unemployment and underemployment. The unemployed are often educated, but trained for jobs that do not exist. While the formal wage sector is absorbing an increasingly smaller proportion of school leavers, education and training often fail to address the realities of the situation facing most young people. These include the need to be able to create or improve their own economic opportunities.

ILO Convention No. 142 – Human Resources Development, 1975, and Recommendation No. 150 – can provide the basis for policy development and legislation. The aim of the convention is to promote the quality and quantity of vocational guidance and training, thus enabling 'all persons to develop and use their capabilities for work in their own best interests, taking into account the needs of society'. Recommendation No. 150 includes a section on the training and employment of women, with suggested measures to promote women's access to education and training for all types of occupation at all levels. The importance of such access was repeatedly stressed at the Nairobi International Women's Conference in 1985, when many delegates identified job segregation as one of the most serious obstacles to the advancement of women.

The workplace is important as an environment for both formal and informal training, and presents the opportunity to negotiate agreements that address the barriers to women's equality. Such agreements may be part of equal opportunities programmes or schemes to revalue occupations and narrow the wage gap between men and women. They could include gender-awareness training for labour inspectors to ensure the implementation of equality legislation, where applicable. In some countries there has been an increase in special training opportunities for women stuck in job ghettos. In Finland women

may, at the employer's expense, prepare for examinations that give them a chance of advancement; trade unions in Norway organize special training for women in female-dominated sectors. The North American unions run a number of courses as part of their career development programmes: the American Federation of State, County and Municipal Employees (AFSCME) has negotiated a package with various public authority employers which includes career counselling, training, and help with job-seeking. The Service Employees International Union (SEIU) has initiated a system whereby local branches establish 'career ladders' for women members; these include job descriptions, a list of skills needed for each job, and information on training facilities.[23]

The OECD stresses that it is important for women's training to focus on sectors of change and growth in order to maximize women's options. Training should also respond to the different needs of different women, and the varying needs of the same woman at different points in her life cycle. Their needs might be: to gain access to higher grades and pay; to keep up with, or benefit from the opportunities of, technical change; to have a wider choice of jobs, including non-traditional occupations; to ease re-entry after absence from the labour market.[24] Training should also fit in with women's responsibilities and timetables.

SKILLS AND VALUE SYSTEMS What sort of skills are needed? They are not just technical but 'life skills': awareness-raising; confidence-building; negotiation; problem-solving; self- and people-management. The strongest barrier to women's social and economic emancipation consists of values and attitudes: not just the attitudes of men or the community but the attitudes of women themselves. Paulo Freire, the Brazilian activist–educator, once said:

THE INTERNATIONAL FEDERATION OF UNIVERSITY WOMEN

International NGOs have not only played an important role in the provision of training but have also contributed to policy development in both formal and informal education. A number of international federations, with member associations in industrialized and developing countries, make use of their local contacts to engage in practical ways with the community, and employ their combined strength to put pressure on governments and international agencies. The International Federation of University Women (IFUW), for example, with members in fifty countries, aims to promote education, the status of women, and international exchange and understanding. The promotion of equal educational opportunity for girls is a high priority.

The national associations in India, the Philippines, Thailand, Turkey and Zimbabwe run literacy classes, and stress the broader aim of enhancing women's participation in development.

The Dutch, French and German associations run campaigns to encourage women to engage in maths, science, computer technology and engineering. The American association has a programme to promote lifelong education and self-development, and the Korean association runs a special school for senior citizens. The Pakistan association founded the Institute of Vocational and Educational Guidance for Girls, in Peshawar.

At its 1986 triennial conference, the federation passed a resolution recommending national associations to lobby governments over women's access to agricultural training, tools and technology.[31] The current theme for study and action is 'Women's future, world future: education for survival and progress'. In its work in preparation for the 1995 Fourth World Conference on Women in Beijing, IFUW is focusing on the girl child as a means of addressing key issues relating to women.

Self-deprecation is a characteristic of the oppressed.... So often do they hear that they are good for nothing, know nothing, and are incapable of learning anything that in the end they become convinced of their own unfitness.[25]

Changing this prepares the ground for the acquisition of vocational, entrepreneurial and managerial skills that can transform a woman's situation. It has become especially clear in the training of women for management that one of the most effective approaches is to set in motion a process of personal development for those concerned.

Attempts to transform the structures of education and employment need to tackle a further issue: the values that society attaches to various skills. The very concept of skill may seem objective, but it is not, because what counts as a skill is the result of very subjective processes. Different pay rates in, for example, the metal and the clothing industries say less about the requirements of the respective jobs than about society's values.[26] Gender bias in defining and valuing skills is so strong that, almost by definition, the work women do is unskilled. The influx of women into an occupation, for example, tends to have the effect of downgrading it, as happened with medicine in the former Soviet Union. Reassessing the skills content of occupations is a process that needs to take place not only at the workplace (see Chapter 7) but also in the education system.

PHOTO: UNICEF/VILAS

The role of non-formal education: a literacy class in India

NON-FORMAL TRAINING ☐ There has been more emphasis here on the formal institutions of learning because these form the basis of a country's public education and training system, and have an indirect as well as direct impact on the access of women to the labour market. It is necessary, however, to appreciate how important non-formal opportunities are for many women, given the extent to which they are still excluded from or disadvantaged in school and vocational training.

For millions of women, education outside the established formal system will be their only route to literacy. It is not good enough to wait for girls' slowly increasing school attendance to affect the literacy figures; women need the chance now to gain the basic skills in literacy and numeracy that can transform the terms on which they relate to the world. Literacy is being more and more interpreted as the gaining of life skills, awareness and bargaining power, not just the ability to read familiar texts from a well-worn primer. This has meant reviewing the content of what is learnt, the methodology used, the role of post-literacy, and the linking of training to employment and/or income-generating opportunities.[27]

Gaps and contradictions persist, however, between theory and practice, and between stated and real commitment to improving the situation of women. Despite the potential importance of non-formal literacy and vocational training not simply to disadvantaged women but to the whole development process, it is a low priority for many governments, especially in comparison with higher education. The lack of resources for training teachers and providing materials reduces the scope and availability of literacy training and undermines its functional aspects. The Education World Literacy Program, UNESCO's experimental effort in the 1970s, relied exclusively on government agencies to implement it. Evaluations showed that the state's presumed advantage in promoting literacy did not materialize. Commitment was weak, co-ordination poor, curricula were insensitive to local needs, and few adults were actually reached.[28] As argued in a UNESCO symposium on women and literacy, there is a clear need to explore parallel organizations, including NGOs.

These groups provide tailored programmes, a greater degree of community participation ... and certainly greater outreach. ... Some women-run NGOs ... have more theoretical clarity than many government projects, [and] are more likely and able to engage in holistic education for women by combining literacy with productive skills and gender consciousness.[29]

The state must, of course, retain a responsibility for non-formal as for formal education, but in both spheres it should extend its approaches and its partners.

NGOs from all regions and a range of perspectives have useful experiences to share. The popular education movement in Latin America, for example, has gathered strength from the understanding that education is a crucial component of empowerment, and also that education becomes more effective in the context of mobilization and group action. In this approach, both education and organization start 'from the lived experiences of participants ... using these known realities as a jumping-off point'.[30]

Adult education is distinguished from vocational training in most industrialized countries, and may be provided by statutory bodies as well as NGOs. It offers opportunities from self-development to civic awareness, as well as the chance to gain further qualifications. School boards in a number of Canadian provinces have appointed Affirmative Action Officers to develop programmes within general adult education provision that will be of particular benefit to women. They cover a wide range of activities including the following:

- career planning, communications and leadership
- vocational training in non-traditional occupations
- gender awareness courses for teachers and trainers
- programmes to ease the transition from home to workplace
- education in parenting.[32]

Many women's groups stress the importance of women informing and educating themselves about the issues and institutions that affect them, and of sharing information with others. Self-education, on an individual or small-group basis, is an option with a long and honourable history. One example is the formation of 'study circles' that spread in the Nordic countries from the late nineteenth century with the aim of creating an educated, and politically and socially committed, working class. These circles, meeting in homes or workplaces with no teachers and few materials, helped people to learn on the basis of their practical experience. They had an important multiplier effect and the methodology has been widely adapted for use in other situations. Trade union education also builds on a long tradition of workers' education, and has given many people a second chance for education as well as transmitting more specifically union-related skills. The expansion in women's education programmes has been particularly significant in promoting equal opportunities within the unions and at work (see Chapter 8).

C **ONCLUSION** ☐ Change can be hard to see because it starts with the attitudes of women themselves to their situation and to the possibilities open to them.

We realise that the future is in our hands. We can influence our children, their schools, other parents so that

attitudes start to change. My daughter is already growing up in a different world from the one I knew. I often had no time for my homework because of the help I had to give in the house.
ZAMBIAN TRADE UNION EDUCATOR[33]

Achievements for women in education and training have been mixed; the increased numbers of women receiving education and training are encouraging, but the concentration of women in certain fields of study, and the higher status of fields where men predominate, remain fixed features and reinforce occupational segregation. Positive action measures are therefore needed, not only within the education system but in the employment sector, with policy-makers, parents and community leaders. Women must be actively involved

throughout this process, not simply viewed as a target.

A range of external factors may possibly provide conditions to favour positive, qualitative change, in particular the need for new skills as a number of sectors restructure, and the promotion of self-employment and small businesses. These are, however, opportunities rather than certainties and, as UNIDO warns, could work against the interests of women unless positive action is taken to help them meet the new requirements.[34]

Finally, it has already been suggested that women will not have truly equal access to the world of work until the very concept of work is rethought. The same is true of the concept of education – since the two are mutually reinforcing – and the values given to different types of institution, methodology, qualification and skill.

1. WOMANKIND, *Women and Education*, WOMANKIND Worldwide, London, n.d., p. 10.
2. United Nations, *The World's Women: Trends and Statistics, 1970–1990*, United Nations, New York, 1991.
3. Ibid.
4. World Bank, *Gender and Poverty in India*, World Bank, Washington, 1991.
5. United Nations.
6. Ibid.
7. Jeanne Vickers, *Women and the World Economic Crisis*, Women and World Development Series, Zed Books, London, 1991.
8. Malcolm Gladwell, 'Who says males are better at maths?', *Way Forum*, April/May/June 1993.
9. ILO, 'Technical background paper for Tripartite Symposium on Equality of Opportunity and Treatment for Men and Women in Employment in Industrialised Countries', ILO, Geneva, 1990.
10. Agnete Andersen, 'The way ahead in Denmark', in *Social Europe*, 3/91 (special issue on equal opportunities for women and men), Commission of the European Communities, pp. 113–14.
11. Vasudha Dhagamwar, 'Education as a tool of ensuring equality for women in employment', report to ILO Equality of Rights branch, ILO, Geneva, n.d.
12. Gretchen Goodale, 'Female access to vocational education and training', in *International Encyclopaedia of Education*, Pergamon, Oxford, forthcoming.
13. ILO, *Namibian Women and Employment: Documents of a Tripartite Symposium*, ILO, Geneva, 1992.
14. International Confederation of Free Trade Unions (ICFTU), *Equality – the Continuing Challenge: Strategies for Success*, Report of the Fifth World Women's Conference, ICFTU, Brussels, 1991.
15. Goodale.
16. Debbie Budlender, *Human Resource Development and Gender Affirmative Action*, Community Agency for Social Enquiry, Johannesburg, n.d.

17. Organisation for Economic Co-operation and Development (OECD), *Shaping Structural Change: the Role of Women*, OECD, Paris, 1991.
18. Goodale.
19. Gretchen Goodale, personal communication.
20. Commonwealth Association of Polytechnics in Africa (CAPA), *Women in Technical Trades*, ILO, Geneva, 1990.
21. UNIDO, *Women and Human Resource Development for Industry*, UNIDO, Vienna, 1988.
22. ILO/UNDP, *A Comprehensive Women's Employment Strategy for Indonesia*, ILO Regional Office for Asia and the Pacific, Bangkok, 1993.
23. Public Services International (PSI), *Paths to Power*, background paper for Second World Women's Conference, PSI, Ferney-Voltaire, 1992.
24. OECD.
25. Quoted in PSI.
26. Budlender.
27. Marcela Ballara, *Women and Literacy*, Women and World Development Series, Zed Books, London, 1991.
28. Nelly Strömqvist, 'Challenges to the attainment of women's literacy', in UNESCO, *Women and Literacy: Yesterday, Today and Tomorrow*. Report of the symposium, Institute of International Education, Stockholm University, 1992.
29. Ibid.
30. Rachael Kamel (ed.), *Growing Together: Women, Feminism and Popular Education*, ISIS International, Rome, 1988.
31. United Nations Educational, Scientific and Cultural Organization (UNESCO), *Women's Education Looks Forward: Programmes, Experiences, Strategies*, UNESCO, Paris, 1989.
32. Ibid.
33. Eva Kolala, personal communication.
34. UNIDO.

7 LABOUR STANDARDS, LAWS AND TRADE UNION ACTION

The issue now is that women should gain the power to change the conditions of working life so that they suit both men and women... [It] is not only a question of making way for the female half of the population, but of creating space for the 'female' side of every individual, men included.

SWEDISH TRADE UNION CENTRE, TCO[1]

THE PROCESS OF DEVELOPING and implementing international labour standards may seem far removed from the everyday working lives of women, but this is where it both starts and ends. It is the issues identified at the workplace that provide the impetus for setting standards. The International Labour Organisation is the United Nations' specialized agency on labour. It provides the means for the social partners – workers, employers and governments – to come together to look into issues of concern, to develop a labour convention if applicable, and then to promote its implementation. Trade unions, employers' associations and national governments all have the right to initiate this process, which is not just a matter of responding to problems but also the means of spreading good ideas and good practice from one country to another.

Many working women have been empowered by these standards:

- The existence of international conventions relating specifically to women legitimizes women's concerns and is a recognition of their place in the labour force.

- Standards provide a guideline for action. They help women workers and their organizations to focus on areas of particular concern, and provide a target to aim at.

- The monitoring processes that examine the implementation of conventions are a source of useful information, and provide a means by which trade unions can exert pressure on governments.

- Even to women outside the organized sector, the standards can provide a declaration of the rights of women workers whatever their situation. International agencies, especially the ILO, are concentrating on ways of extending the application of standards to the agricultural and informal sectors.

THE INTERNATIONAL LABOUR OR-GANISATION ☐ The International Labour Organisation (ILO) was set up in 1919 to improve living and working conditions and to promote social justice. In order to achieve this, it brings together representatives of governments, employers and workers. It is the only organization in the United Nations with members from outside government; they have full voting rights.

The main activity of the ILO is to set international labour standards, in the form of conventions and recommendations, and to supervise how they are being applied at national level. Other activities cover a wide variety of areas, including:

- collecting, analysing, and disseminating information on social and labour matters;

- organizing meetings to work out new ideas and principles;
- providing services to member states including technical assistance and workers' education.

INTERNATIONAL STANDARDS By 1 January 1993, a total of 173 conventions and 178 recommendations had been adopted. These instruments provide guidelines for legislators and a stimulus for action on working conditions, industrial relations, and the protection and promotion of basic human rights, which include equality of opportunity and treatment for women.

Conventions Conventions are international treaties setting standards for all aspects of work. When a country formally agrees to a convention, this is known as ratification.

The ILO also adopts recommendations, which do not impose binding obligations but may supplement points made in a convention and provide guidelines for national policy and action. To help countries understand and apply standards, especially the more important and wide-ranging ones, the ILO undertakes education programmes around the major issues of concern and reinforces them through technical co-operation programmes.

Ratification and implementation Once a convention is ratified the government concerned must make regular reports to the ILO on the measures it has taken to apply it. Even in the case of an unratified convention, governments may be called upon to report on the relevant law and practice in their countries, and to explain what is preventing or delaying its ratification. The trade unions and employers' associations are entitled to receive copies of these reports and to comment on them.

The women's committee of the Zambian Congress of Trade Unions and the women's wing of the United National Independence Party combined forces to put pressure on the government to ratify Conventions Nos. 111 and 100, supported by the fact that the government would need to explain to the ILO why Zambia, unlike an increasing number of other African countries, had not achieved ratification.

Supervisory machinery The reports from governments on ratified Conventions are examined first by the Committee of Experts on the Application of conventions and Recommendations. The Committee's comments are discussed annually by government, employer and worker representatives at the International Labour Conference. The Committee of Experts also conducts its own surveys: a general survey was carried out in 1986 to review progress being made in member states on equal pay, in 1988 on equality of opportunity and treatment at work, and in 1993 on workers with family responsibilities. These surveys provide interesting overviews of a range of practical initiatives tried by different countries.

Provision also exists for representations and complaints to be made in the case of violation of ratified conventions. These may be made by a national or international workers' organization, or employers' association. They are examined by a committee composed of three members of the Governing Body, one from each of the social partners.

HUMAN RIGHTS ☐ The focus of this chapter is on labour standards, rights and laws, but it is important not to lose sight of other, complementary instruments. The rights of workers are basic human rights, as contained in the Universal Declaration of Human Rights, and the rights of women in particular are taken up in the Convention on the Elimination of

Table 7.1: CALENDAR OF ACTION ON INTERNATIONAL LABOUR STANDARDS
Adoption of conventions and recommendations

PERIOD	ILO ACTION	ACTION BY NATIONAL ADMINISTRATIONS	ACTION BY WOMEN WORKERS
YEAR 1 May and November	ILO Governing Body decides agenda of ILO Conference in Year 3.		Identify problems for women workers and needs for new international labour standards and try to make ILO Governing Body take up the issue as agenda item of ILO Conference through workers' member of the Governing Body.
YEAR 2 June	ILO circulates report on law and practice, with questionnaire.	Prepare replies to question-naire and send to ILO by 30 September, at the latest. The Standing Orders of the Con-ference require governments to consult the most representa-tative employers' and workers' organizations to make comments before final-ising replies to the question-naire.	The law and practice report, as well as questionnaires, are made available to the most representative workers' organisation for their comments. Have workers' observations reflected in or added to replies of government. Or send them to ILO directly.
YEAR 3 February	ILO circulates report analysing replies, with proposed conclusions.	Prepare position for ILO Conference discussion.	Study ILO report and prepare position for ILO Conference discussions.
June	ILO Conference – first discussion of item.	Participate in work of tri-partite technical committee of ILO Conference, as appropriate.	Participate in tripartite technical committee of ILO Conference, as appropriate.
August	ILO circulates draft texts on basis of first discussion.	Study and, if necessary, send comments to ILO by 30 November at the latest. Con-sult with the most representa-tive organisations.	Study and, if necessary, send workers' comments to government or ILO.
YEAR 4 March	ILO circulates revised texts, in light of com-ments received.	Prepare position for ILO Conference discussion.	Study revised texts and pre-pare position for ILO Conference discussion.
June	ILO Conference – second discussion and adoption.	Participate in work of tripartite technical committee of ILO Conference, as appropriate.	Participate in tripartite technical committee of ILO Conference, as appropriate.

All Forms of Discrimination Against Women, usually known as the Women's Convention. This and other United Nations instruments are examined in more detail in two sister volumes in this series, *Women and Human Rights* and *Women and Empowerment*. A number of regional standards have also been established: the Directives of the European Community, for example, have had an important impact on the adoption of laws to promote equality in its member states.

PROMOTING EQUAL OPPORTUNITIES □
All labour standards aim to improve working conditions for all workers, but in recognition of the deeply entrenched and systematic discrimination against women in employment, and the particular demands of their reproductive role, the ILO has approved special instruments to combat discrimination and respond to women's specific needs. The most comprehensive and wide-ranging of the ILO's conventions relating to women (and other groups of workers) is Convention No. 111 – Discrimination (Employment and Occupation) 1958 – and Recommendation No. 111. The aim of the standard is 'to promote equality of opportunity and treatment for employment and occupation', meaning both access to employment and conditions of work. It defines discrimination as 'any distinction, exclusion, or preference made on the basis of race, colour, sex, religion, political opinion, national extraction, or social origin, which has the effect of nullifying or impairing equality of opportunity or treatment in employment or occupation'. Although discrimination on the basis of age is not explicitly mentioned here, the Older Workers' Recommendation, number 162 (1980), includes a section on equality of opportunity and treatment in employment.[2]

> **ILO CONVENTION NO. 111**
> Convention No. 111 specifies that all persons should enjoy equality of opportunity and treatment in respect of:
> - access to vocational guidance and placement services;
> - access to training and employment;
> - advancement in employment;
> - security of tenure;
> - remuneration;
> - hours and conditions of work, as well as social security measures and welfare facilities.

Each state that ratifies the standard must develop a national policy for the prevention of discrimination and the promotion of equality of opportunity. This includes abolishing or changing any laws or practices that are not in line with this policy. A national agency or authority should be designated to oversee the implementation of the policy and, with employers' and workers' organizations, to ensure the development of educational programmes, vocational guidance, retraining, and placement services. Because Convention No. 111 deals with human rights, states that have ratified it are required to report on its application more frequently than for other conventions. By 1 September 1993 it had received 117 ratifications, among the highest number for any convention.

The last survey on the application of the convention was undertaken by the Committee of Experts in 1988. It found that indirect discrimination, in particular, was slow to be eradicated and stressed the need for all the social partners to take a 'combination of legislative and practical measures' at all levels in order to break down the barriers to equality.[3] In a number of countries a more comprehensive approach is being attempted. The Nordic states have set a notable example in terms of integrating women into the economy. This inte-

gration been associated with public policies supporting gender equity, structural measures such as workplace equal opportunities committees, relatively small wage gaps, and social provisions including childcare facilities and paid leave. In this way a climate of opportunity, indeed encouragement, has been created.

AFFIRMATIVE ACTION National equal opportunities policy and workplace programmes are increasingly based on or include the principle of affirmative action, also called positive action or positive discrimination. This principle is described in the Nairobi *Forward-looking Strategies for the Advancement of Women* as 'special measures designed to redress the imbalance imposed by centuries of discrimination against women ... in order to accelerate equality'.[4] This represents a shift in emphasis from the opposing of discrimination to the active promotion of equality. Measures might include very precise provisions to increase the numbers of women in certain sectors or grades where they are underrepresented, for example by establishing quotas or quantitative targets. They

can also include wide-ranging programmes such as public information to counter stereotypes, advocacy with employers, adjustments to working time and organization, and vocational training, retraining and counselling. An important element is that measures should be part of a plan, with numerical goals and a fixed time frame, and with provisions for reporting and monitoring. This reinforces the principle that affirmative action is a temporary, 'catch-up' strategy whilst equal opportunities in general are a universal right, and as such have a permanent place in employment policy at all levels.

Affirmative action measures are usually the subject of voluntary compliance, but in some countries they are enforced by national or local legislation. The Roudy Law in France lays down rules to promote equality in all aspects of employment from job advertising to pay equity. Each enterprise with more than fifty employees is required to prepare an annual report comparing the situation of men and women in relation to recruitment, training, promotion and working conditions. The reports serve as guidelines for occupational equality plans which set out specific measures, such as reserved posts and quotas for promotion, to accelerate the advancement of women.[5] One outcome has been an agreement between the International Union of Food and Allied Workers (IUF) and the French food multinational BSN which included an action plan to promote equality between men and women at the workplace. The plan will apply not only to the firm's operations in France; it will be extended to plants in Italy, Germany, Spain, Greece and Brazil.[6]

Although it is hard to assess the relative effects of different factors, the success of affirmative action is suggested by the strong representation of women in areas where programmes are well-established: in senior and professional posts in the Canadian public service, for example. A Department of Labor study in the United States found that women's employment increased by 15 per cent in companies with affirmative action goals, but by only 2 per cent in other establishments.[7] In developing countries, nearly all documented initiatives have been in the public sector. In India, for example, measures are being introduced by the federal government to favour women in education, and by some state governments to reserve jobs for women. The State of Andhra Pradesh has given the following directive: 'In recruitment to posts for which women as well as men are equally suited, other things being equal, preference should be given to women.'[8] In Bangladesh between 10 and 15 per cent of government jobs are reserved for women, and women's share of government employment increased from less than 3 per cent in the early 1970s to 8 per cent in 1990.[9]

A recent report on positive action in Zimbabwe found that there had been 'meaningful [and] concrete' developments both in the public service and in areas of education and training managed by the government. A policy of positive discrimination was introduced in 1990 to favour the promotion of women to middle and senior management positions in the civil service. A regional scholarship programme for secondary education reserves 70 per cent of awards for girls, and targets have been established in technical training programmes to increase the enrolment of women from 3 to 10 per cent.

The reaction of women who benefited from the civil service programme was that it was very welcome, but long overdue and not being pushed along fast enough. The male managers were 'easily satisfied with small progress'. Most men interviewed accepted that women had been disadvantaged in the past, and a number welcomed the programme, provided it was short-term and limited in its scope, and that only competent women were promoted. All those who worked with the women concerned agreed that they were up to the task, but some men clearly felt threatened by the whole scheme.[10]

The collective bargaining process also plays a significant role in combating discrimination and establishing equal working conditions, especially where equal opportunities or positive action measures are not legally enforced. It obliges demands to be well-planned and structured, it engages the employer, and it has a built-in sanction in the grievance procedure. To date, however, much of this bargaining has been 'gender-blind' and has perpetuated women's disadvantage or, at best, failed to correct it. There is an urgent need for all collective agreements to be reviewed to ensure that they not only avoid discrimination but actively promote equality.

The British Trades Union Congress (TUC) has produced *More Than You Bargained For: a TUC Negotiator's Pack on Bargaining for Equality*, which shows union representatives how to recognize discrimination and how to initiate bargaining to address various areas of inequality. It

TUC EDUCATION SERVICE

CHECKLIST: Equal Opportunities – a checklist for negotiators

You may find the following questions useful when you're preparing to negotiate, or review, an equal opportunities agreement with your employer:-

1. do you have an Equal Opportunities Agreement?
2. do all members and prospective members know about it?
3. is it published or advertised?
4. is it monitored?
5. is it reviewed by management and union representatives? If so how and how often?
6. does it deal with job segregation, or lack of promotion for women?
7. does it commit management to take positive action where the policy is not working? If so what positive action has been taken and is it showing results?
8. are management and employees trained on the policy? Is the training regularly updated?
9. is there a joint union/employer Equal Opportunities Committee? Does it meet on a regular basis?
10. is there an agreed procedure for investigating complaints about recruitment, appointments and promotions?
11. can staff get paid time off work to attend union training on equal opportunities?
12. does the agreement demand that all collective agreements are reviewed to eliminate any sex bias?

covers nine major areas of concern, explains how women have come to be disadvantaged, advises on ways of gathering relevant information, sets out sample policy statements and outlines action to take within the framework of collective bargaining. The areas covered include pay, training and promotion, working hours, and child care.[11]

PAY INEQUITY □ The gap between men's and women's pay is one aspect of unequal opportunities. This is not simply a technical problem, stemming from the concentration of women in certain occupations and at lower levels of responsibility, but reflects the value given by society to women's skills and work. The solution is unlikely to be total until job segregation has been eliminated, and equality achieved in all aspects of employment. Measures can still be taken, however, to address pay levels in different sectors and

workplaces, in tandem with more wide-ranging equal opportunities programmes. Convention No. 100, Equal Remuneration (1951), and Recommendation No. 90 lay down the principle of equal pay for work of equal value. Pay includes both basic wages and benefits or allowances, in cash or in kind. Ratifying states agree to promote the principle of equal pay for work of equal value and make sure that it is applied to all workers: by means of national laws, wage-fixing machinery, collective agreements, or a combination of measures. The convention specifies 'work of equal value' and not 'equal work', a distinction not generally made in the 1950s, and not universal today. The concept of equal pay for work of equal, or comparable, value or worth is also known as pay equity, particularly in North America.

Recommendation No. 90 encourages governments to ensure that pay equity is applied to its own employees, as well as more generally. Both the convention and the recommendation advocate the establishment of methods to evaluate types of work, with the aim of classifying jobs without regard to sex. The importance of this is not just as a measure for the economic protection of women but as a means of raising the status of women by revaluing women's jobs. This convention has been ratified by 119 member states.

The ratification of Convention No. 100 and the adoption of equal pay legislation had measurable – but one-off – effects on women's pay levels in certain countries. In Japan, for example, the Equal Opportunity in Employment Law of 1985 had an immediate impact on the starting salaries of women college graduates in some sectors. The wage gap tended to narrow in most industrialized countries in the 1960s and 1970s, as more women came onto the job market. It was also found that as a number of countries introduced a minimum wage, this had a great impact on women's pay because so many women were among the badly-paid.[12] Since 1980, however, the wage ratio between men and women has remained static in most countries, worsened in a few – including Brazil, Costa Rica, Sweden and Denmark – and improved most consistently in the United States.[13]

The fact that equal pay clauses have existed in the legislation of many countries for a number of years without a clear closing of the wage gap has led to a review of the processes that establish pay levels. Trade unions have a particular responsibility for maintaining and improving workers' living standards which they address through negotiating on pay and conditions. Fundamental and widespread changes have taken place in bargaining practices which used to increase rather than reduce differentials, ignoring the interests of many workers, such as those on part-time or temporary contracts. When pay increases are based on a percentage of existing pay, for example, the low-paid get less and the gap widens. Negotiators are now increasingly trying to compensate by getting flat-rate increases for the lower wage bands, and also 'equality allowances'. Collective agreement in Finland in 1988 resulted in the establishment of an 'equal pay kitty' for low-paid women workers: a small levy is paid by employers for all women in government offices and then the low-paid receive a greater increase than the well-paid at each pay round.

JOB EVALUATION A more comprehensive approach to the problem has been the attempt to apply the concept of 'work of equal value' across occupational divisions and to use job evaluation techniques to assess job content in a non-discriminatory way. Jobs are evaluated and compared on the basis of skill (training and experience), physical and mental effort, responsibility and working conditions, though the biases and values of society make it difficult for these to be established objectively. Why, for example, is being responsible for people given less value – or at least rewarded less well – than being responsible for a machine? Why are women unable to lift heavy weights in an industrial setting, but able in a hospital, kindergarten or the home? A number of elements are necessary in order to make this approach work, including:

- the development of job and skills evaluation criteria that are gender-neutral;

- mechanisms specifically designed to deal with sex discrimination;

- training of negotiators and the appointment of more women negotiators;

- updating of job classifications;

PHOTO: ILO/J. MAILLARD

A range of measures needs to be taken to combat the concentration of women in low-paid jobs

- ensuring that pay legislation and collective agreements specify 'work of equal or comparable value'.

EQUAL PAY IN THE USA

Jobs judged in the USA to have the same value include a cook and a car mechanic, a typing pool supervisor and a radio communications supervisor. Following judgements such as these, trade unions have launched many claims for pay increases on the basis of the new valuations.

The public sector union AFSCME, for example, has negotiated over half a billion dollars in pay equity adjustments through a combination of collective bargaining, legislation, and litigation.[14]

THE WAY FORWARD? Canada is in the forefront of legislation on pay equity. Five provinces have proactive legislation that puts the onus on the employer to implement pay equity whether or not there has been a complaint. Two other provinces require proactive procedures but through the collective bargaining process rather than regulation. In general, the application of these laws is limited to public employees (staff in the education and health services as well as municipal and central government). In Ontario, however, there has been a breakthrough into the private sector, starting with large companies, giving it 'the leading edge in Canada – indeed in the world – in that it has both proactive legislation and applies [it] to the private as well as the public sector'.[15]

It is significant that a number of measures have been initiated by state authorities and/or public service unions, and also that the wage gap is often smaller in the public than the private sector – the difference is over 10 per cent in the USA, for example. The state has a role in establishing national equality policies as well as setting an example of good practice as an employer, so it is worrying that some data suggest a slow-down in the trend towards pay equality in the public service.[16]

MATERNITY RIGHTS AND PROTECTION □

Women come into the labour force both as workers and as women. Maternity protection is essential to the achievement of equal opportunities in order to ensure that women are not disadvantaged in relation to their biological functions of child-bearing and breast-feeding. It also has a special place in development because of the positive impact on women of ante- and post-natal care and on children if they can be breast-fed for at least four months. There are also spin-off effects in terms of family planning.

The third convention ever adopted by the ILO was an instrument to protect women workers in respect of child-bearing. It was revised in 1952 to respond to changes in working practice: Convention No. 103 – Maternity Protection (revised) (1952) – and Recommendation No. 95 cover the issues of protection against dismissal, conditions at work for pregnant women, paid leave and medical care, and breaks for nursing a child. Thirty member states have ratified the convention.

The survey of the application of the convention carried out in 1982 found that maternity arrangements had been broadened or reinforced in a large number of countries over the previous decade, that dismissal of pregnant women was widely outlawed, and that the categories of women excluded from maternity protection were being steadily reduced. Allowances for nursing breaks are increasingly included in workplace agreements. Collective bargaining is widely used in order to extend the provisions of the law, or even to put them into practice. In Japan, for example, the law provides for sixteen weeks' leave, but it depends on negotiation whether this is paid or not. A review in 1993 of national laws relating to maternity protection noted significant progress in the duration of maternity leave and in cash benefits. A growing awareness that women should not be disadvantaged in the labour market on account of maternity has led a number of countries to introduce measures to ensure that women do not suffer discrimination on the grounds of pregnancy. This review might lead to a further revision of the standard.

It has to be recognized, however, that the notion of maternity protection sometimes works against the interests of the very women it seeks to protect: because of the leave provisions and associated cost, some employers are reluctant to hire women of child-bearing age, or insist on pregnancy tests or even sterilization certificates.

In a number of urban slum areas in Brazil, where women have no other source of income, between 50 and 80 per cent of women between the ages of fifteen and fifty-four have been sterilized, many of whom had not had any children.[17] Evidence has also come to light that in some factories in the Dominican Republic, pills are distributed which cause sterility.[18]

For this reason, the standard sets out the principle that maternity pay or benefits must be provided through a social security scheme or government funds, and that employers should not be individually liable. In many countries, however, social security schemes are underdeveloped or over-stretched, so the employer does have to pay. It is therefore essential for new forms of shared cost or social insurance systems to be devised. In Burkina Faso, the unions on the tripartite governing body of the social security department have secured an agreement that working mothers will be covered by social security during their three months' leave. 'This has reassured employers who no longer hesitate to hire young women and who can replace their staff member by a temporary worker,' said Mamounata Cissé of the Organisation

National des Syndicats Libres (ONSL).[19] Legal action is also being taken to oppose abuses by employers. In Venezuela, for example, the 1990 Labour Act prohibits pregnancy testing by employers during recruitment.

FAMILY RESPONSIBILITIES ☐ Many women find that their greatest problem in holding down a job outside the home is the fact that they must fit a range of domestic tasks into their day as well. ILO Convention No. 156 – Workers with Family Responsibilities (1981) – along with Recommendation No. 165 is interesting because of the assumptions it challenges and the possibilities it suggests. It recognizes that workers who are responsible for children or other family members (a sick or elderly person, for example) may have difficulties in carrying out their jobs. Ratifying states must make it possible for these people to work without discrimination but, what is more, they should help eliminate the conflict between their employment and family responsibilities by promoting workplace and community planning measures to respond to the needs of workers with families. The fact that the convention speaks of workers, and not just women, makes it clear that family responsibilities should be shared by men and women; the recommendation spotlights the role of the state in providing services that are free or of reasonable cost. This standard has stimulated and reinforced action on a number of different fronts. The two main spheres of action are working arrangements, especially different forms of leave, and the provision of child care and family services. It also encourages a strategy of information and education to promote public awareness. The role of training and retraining is covered, as is the use of social security in relation to leave and home-based responsibilities. Twenty member states have ratified this convention.

A survey on the policies and programmes of countries to implement the convention was completed in 1992, and the results were presented in a report by the Committee of Experts on the Application of Conventions and Standards to the Eightieth Session of the International Labour Conference (1993). This 'was gratified to note' the many measures being actively fostered to improve both conditions of work and the sharing of domestic responsibilities. Country reports showed many examples of practical measures to facilitate the entry or re-entry to employment of workers with family responsibilities; innovations in the arrangement of working time; more widespread parental leave; and 'significant progress in the development of child-care services and facilities, and some improvements as regards family services and facilities'. The Committee of Experts also noted that employers who have adopted 'family-friendly' policies and facilities report positive changes in the workplace including: improved morale; lower absenteeism and staff turnover; easier staff recruitment; and favourable publicity and community relations.[20]

LEAVE ARRANGEMENTS The standard provides for either parent to have leave of absence immediately after the period of maternity leave; this is known as parental leave. It is restricted to the first year of a child's life in most countries, though it is available until the child is three in France and Spain. Some countries enable workers to combine parental leave with part-time working. Normally this leave is unpaid, but workers retain occupational seniority and pension rights; in some countries allowances are made through the social security system. Under the Swedish Equal Opportunities Act, employers have to take measures that actively encourage take-up by fathers.[21]

Harmony between employment and family responsibilities

Paternity leave is a short leave period given to new fathers which is becoming increasingly widespread, though more often as a clause in a collective agreement than in the national law. Three trade unions in Namibia advocate paternity leave of between two and four weeks after the birth of a child. While acknowledging that fathers are unlikely to participate directly in child care, they believe that men would lighten the mother's load by helping around the house during this period.[22]

Many arrangements, formal and informal, exist to cope with the occasional crisis which may crop up in any family. The standard stipulates that leave provisions should be made for these eventualities, rather than employees having to take sick leave or make *ad hoc* arrangements with supervisors. Some countries make provisions in law on the basis of days per year, or per illness; these are usually paid. In Norway, for example, both parents have the right to ten days' leave a year in the event of children's illness or domestic problems; in Finland a worker with a sick child under ten may be absent for up to four consecutive days, and longer with a doctor's certificate. In certain countries, parents also have the right to a reduction in working hours until their children reach a certain age.

CHILD CARE Whatever arrangements can be made in terms of leave and flexible working, there will always be the need for safe and affordable arrangements for the care of children, both before schooling starts and in tandem with school life. The principal requirements are that the care should be reliable and of good quality, affordable, conveniently located, and at hours that match working schedules. Child care is an issue in every sector; indeed the lack of care is a factor in the rise of some forms of employment, such as homeworking, as well as in informal activities and

self-employment. Child care responsibilities also make it more difficult for women to follow training, get involved in trade unions, or enjoy leisure and recreation.

The Committee of Experts' report shows that child care provision has increased and improved in many countries, although figures are rarely available for the extent of unmet demand. While more public provision exists in industrialized countries, sometimes subsidized or tax-deductible, facilities in developing countries are often privately provided and expensive. The extensive facilities in the former Communist countries are being rapidly dismantled. Where provision is particularly good, as in the Nordic countries, this is usually because it is part of a wider policy of equality of opportunity and treatment, and broad social objectives. Indeed, the ILO recommends that child care should be linked into broader social and community planning. The report also notes that an increasing number of initiatives are coming from the employers.

Child care is not only becoming more widely available, but it is also gradually becoming more responsive to the needs of workers: for facilities for babies and older children outside school, for example, and also for night care and special assistance if a child is ill. Ideally, families should have a choice of care in the home, in the community or in the workplace. Services provided by local authorities may include information and referral as well as actual care. Governments can help defray costs for the employer and worker through tax relief and should be encouraged to do so, in acknowledgement of the fact that provisions benefit industry and society as well as the individual. Similarly, employers should contribute to community-based facilities. Child care facilities increased rapidly in the Netherlands and New Zealand following the negotiation of state subsidies: in New Zealand for the capital costs and in the

Netherlands for wages – provided they were for previously unemployed workers. Women, of course, have made ingenious informal arrangements for years, and probably always will. NGOs have also made an active contribution in providing facilities, often in association with income-generation, literacy or training schemes, recognizing their importance to women's self-reliance.

Most trade unions now have child care firmly on their agendas, and may negotiate for workplace facilities or a child care allowance depending on circumstances. Some have set up their own schemes, usually linked to specific events such as courses or meetings, but in Fiji, for example, a full-time child care programme has been started by unions for their members, and similarly in Uganda. A number of unions stress that child care is a social issue, not a women's issue. In Germany, for example, the identification of women's issues with family issues has been rejected, and separate policies and strategies are pursued to deal with family and social matters and with women's rights.

'WORKERS ARE PARENTS TOO!'
September 20 1990 was a day of action organized by the Congress of South African Trade Unions (COSATU). Workers took their children with them to factories, shops and offices in order to make a clear point about the lack of childcare facilities. Many men took part, as part of the objective was to challenge the notion that children are the mother's responsibility alone.[23]

PROTECTION OR EQUALITY? ☐ The earliest standards established by the ILO to improve working conditions for women concentrated on their protection rather than the promotion of equality, though at the time these were pioneering. Examples include the Maternity Protection Convention (1919, revised in 1952), the Night Work (Women) Convention (1919,

revised in 1934, 1948 and 1990), and the Underground Work (Women) Convention (1935). Other standards relate to the manual transport of loads and to the handling of poisonous substances, including exposure to lead and radiation. In some cases the protection is specifically intended for pregnant women and in others for all women. Some of these instruments have become controversial or simply outdated in the course of the years, and a number of governments have begun to consider the restrictions they impose on women's employment as obstacles to their access to certain jobs and therefore discriminatory. Other governments, and workers' bodies in particular, argue that the way forward is not to repeal the measures that protect women but to extend them to cover all workers.[24]

NIGHT WORK A lot of debate has centred on the Night Work (Women) Convention, No. 89 (revised 1948), which has been 'denounced' by fifteen governments – meaning that the countries concerned have withdrawn their ratifications. They argue that the prohibition on working at night in factories (services are exempt) may deprive women of the opportunity to take part in overtime, productivity bonus, and flexible hours schemes. Also, more basically, it limits women's freedom of choice. On the other hand, the effects of night working on health are generally negative, for men and for women, and unions warn that companies want women night workers not for the sake of equality but for flexibility and lower wages.

As a result of this debate, a solution has been found that offers the possibility both of compromise and of improving conditions for all night workers. A protocol has been added to Convention No. 89 which permits certain exemptions; a new convention has also been agreed, No. 171 (1990), which applies both to men and to women who work at night. Its provisions are designed to protect the health, safety, family and social responsibilities, and advancement of night workers, with special provisions for pregnant women. Governments may now choose between ratifying the new convention and ratifying or maintaining Convention No. 89, with or without the Protocol.

HEALTH AND SAFETY: OTHER ISSUES

□ The question of health and safety should be considered in as broad a context as possible, and areas identified where protective measures need to be increased rather than reduced. It is also important that those activities and environments that have a detrimental effect on the health and safety of women in particular should be identified and addressed. A number of the jobs where women predominate expose them to particular health risks, as noted above in electronics and plantation work. Another example is nursing, which involves much heavy lifting though maximum weight restrictions do not apply. A number of health problems are associated with repetitive work, often involving women, from assembly line production to computer-operating. Women also tend to be overrepresented in occupations that are stressful or have stressful aspects to them, including a lack of control over one's work and environment; low job satisfaction; and insecurity of contract. Another point of stress is the pressure to reconcile domestic and workplace responsibilities.

ENFORCING HEALTH AND SAFETY STANDARDS

Laws based on the various health and safety conventions are quite widespread and machinery is in place to ensure compliance in a number of countries. Many countries have an occupational health and safety division or authority, and networks of health and safety or labour inspectors exist to monitor conditions in places of work. Almost invariably, how-ever, there are not enough inspectors to do the job adequately and in a number of countries resources do not run to such a system. This is why it is particularly important that workplace health and safety officers should be appointed from the workforce; where a workplace is unionized, these officers are normally appointed by the union, and health and safety training is an important part of union education. In respect to certain hazards, especially pesticides, and certain sectors of work, NGOs and women's associations have been particularly active in bringing problems to public view and putting pressure on the relevant authorities.

Health and safety measures need not just be defensive: the workplace also provides the opportunity to arrange health education and take preventive measures such as screening for cervical cancer.[25]

VIOLENCE AGAINST WOMEN

□ The violence suffered by women at home, in the streets and at work is at last starting to be seen as a violation of human rights, a social and not a personal problem.[26] It is this issue more than any other which has been an impetus and rallying point for many Third World women's organizations, and that has come to represent women's common oppression in both North and South. In 1993, the Commission on the Status of Women agreed a draft Declaration on Violence against Women, which will go before the United Nations General Assembly for adoption. It is also starting to be recognized that wherever violence takes place, if it affects working people then it is an issue which workers and their organizations should address. In 1990, the Canadian Labour Congress launched a particularly high-profile campaign to combat violence against women, and a federal law has now been passed which clarifies the definition of violence and establishes legal redress. Trade unions in other coun-

The importance of occupational health standards

tries have taken up issues such as domestic violence and violence at work.[27]

SEXUAL HARASSMENT Sexual harassment at work is one form of violence against women, a health and safety matter as well as an issue of human rights. The influx of women into the workforce over the past twenty years has both magnified the problem and enabled women to be more vocal in their own defence. An increasing number of surveys suggest that the majority of women have suffered some form of harassment in the course of their work. Sexual harassment can be defined as unwanted sexual advances – by word, look or gesture – that cause offence or distress to the person at whom they are aimed. They can range from jokes and touching to blackmail and physical assault.

Harassment in a general sense is one example of discrimination: a group or individual with more power or confidence picks on a weaker group or individual. Sexual harassment is a form of victimization that stems from the lack of equality between the sexes, and that emphasizes sexual differences. The victims are usually, though not only, women: grandmothers as well as young, single women. Sexual harassment is less about straightforward sex than about power. Those responsible are often men in a position of authority over the person they are harassing. Certain groups of women are particularly vulnerable: for example live-in domestic workers, and also women who work in non-traditional, male-dominated occupations: the lone woman on a building site, for example. This undermines the breaking down of job segregation and the promotion of equal opportunities. Victims may suffer in a number of ways, feeling stress and anxiety, isolation and even guilt. Other effects can include loss of promotion, an unwanted transfer, or loss of a job. If the situation becomes public, it can cause emotional reactions and divide a workplace.

Sexual harassment remains an extremely sensitive matter and one many people find difficult to discuss. It has been acknowledged as a serious workplace issue only relatively recently in industrialized countries, and in other regions, where women have come into the labour force more recently and in smaller numbers, it is not surprising that there should still be either denial of the problem or reluctance to report incidents. Participants at women's trade union seminars frequently report that they have never been able to discuss sexual harassment in public before.

Measures taken to deal with the problem include: additions and amendments to laws; workplace agreements; and trade union training. The Canadian Human Rights Act has a clause making it clear that 'harassment is considered to have taken place if a reasonable person ought to have known such behaviour is unwelcome'. In some countries employers can be taken to court for permitting sexual harassment to take place. Awareness-raising at workplaces and through trade unions has been found to be an effective form of prevention. Company and union policy statements on sexual harassment help create a climate where harassment is viewed as unacceptable, while the mere existence of procedures to support victims and sanction aggressors can result in a beneficial shift in the balance of power.

SEXUAL HARASSMENT: A TANZANIAN SOLUTION

In Tanzania a series of awareness-raising meetings and workshops culminated in the setting up of the Committee Against Sexual Harassment, Discrimination, and Violence. The committee brings together professional women, trade unionists and community activists 'to enhance the struggle and safeguard the rights of women and children'. It has set up working groups to deal with the legal and medical aspects of sexual harassment and rape; to counsel and support victims; and to offer legal advice to women who face discrimination at work.[28]

MAKING THE LAW WORK FOR WOMEN

□ If the implementation of labour legislation depends in large part on the organization of labour, the motivation of trade unions to bargain on the basis of equal opportunities legislation is, in turn, largely dependent on the involvement of women in the unions and on pressure from them. It is critical not only that women should participate in trade unions, but that they should understand the issues involved and how to apply pressure.

> Transformation of the situation of working women rests on three pillars: laws that establish equality principles; women's active participation in workers' organizations, and women's understanding of their rights.

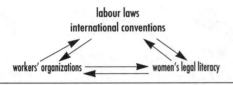

labour laws
international conventions

workers' organizations ⟶ women's legal literacy

LEGAL LITERACY PROGRAMMES

It has been well said that a law that no one knows about does not really exist. Legal literacy is about bridging the gap between the statute book and the people it concerns: without the involvement of the people there is not only no implementation, but no law. The principles of legal literacy are that, first, people should know their rights and, second, they should have the means to defend and enforce them. The objective is equality in practice, not just in law, meaning equal access to and control over resources and opportunities, and not simply equal 'status'. The need to help women understand and exercise their rights is widely recognized, and programmes have been put in place worldwide. These range from the training of a corps of paralegal workers in Nigeria, legal aid 'surgeries' run by community lawyers in Australia, and rural legal aid camps in India, to legal empowerment through popular education in Latin America

and the government-run Programme for Acquainting Citizens with Basic Knowledge of Law in China.[29]

It is necessary to distinguish between the situation where women are deprived of their rights because these are not established in law, and where the problem is that formal rights exist but women cannot exercise them in practice. In the first case action must be taken to change the law, in the second to implement existing laws.[30] International labour standards have a special role to play in both cases. If the law needs to be changed, women can press for the ratification of relevant standards, because legal adjustments will then follow. This pressure can be exerted through workers' organizations, and in partnership with other NGOs and associations which can mobilize different sections of public opinion. Most standards also contain recommendations for implementation, and governments are required to submit regular progress reports. Any individual workers' or employers' organization can also submit reports detailing lack of action, or even overt violation of standards.

HOW TO IMPLEMENT LABOUR STANDARDS

If we, women workers, feel that our country is neglecting its commitment to positive labour legislation in spite of ratification, what can we do?

1. You can draw the attention of the ILO's Committee of Experts to the matter. You can require the inclusion of your comments in the government's report to the Committee of Experts, or you can send a letter to the ILO for the attention of the Committee of Experts.

2. You can make a formal representation through your national trade union, or international union body, which will be considered by the ILO's Governing Body.

3. You can get advice and assistance from the Adviser on International Labour Standards in the nearest ILO Regional Office, or from ILO headquarters.[31]

MAKING THE LAW WORK FOR WOMEN
Challenging the Legal System

INTERNATIONAL WOMEN'S TRIBUNE CENTRE

Here are some ideas for challenging or using each of the components outlined to empower women socially, economically and politically. Together, these challenges form a strategy for changing the law and the legal system that could be formidable.

Watch out! We are going to change many things!

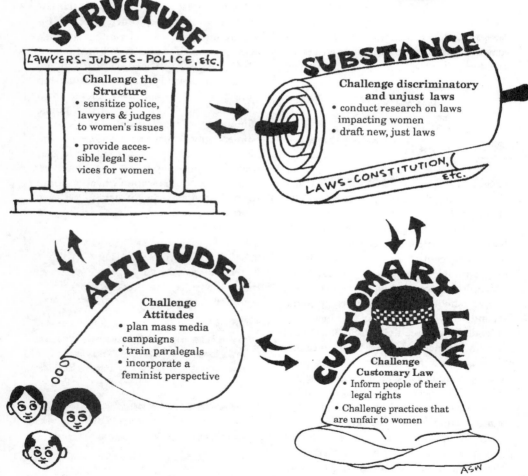

STRUCTURE

LAWYERS - JUDGES - POLICE, etc.

Challenge the Structure
• sensitize police, lawyers & judges to women's issues

• provide accessible legal services for women

SUBSTANCE

Challenge discriminatory and unjust laws
• conduct research on laws impacting women
• draft new, just laws

LAWS - CONSTITUTION, etc.

ATTITUDES

Challenge Attitudes
• plan mass media campaigns
• train paralegals
• incorporate a feminist perspective

CUSTOMARY LAW

Challenge Customary Law
• Inform people of their legal rights

• Challenge practices that are unfair to women

ASW

CONCLUSION ☐ At an ILO workshop in Tanzania on women in rural workers' organizations, the programme had to be rewritten after participants had a session on international labour standards. Such was their interest in the role of the standards, and how they related to equality issues and the day-to-day challenge of organizing in rural areas, that the women asked for more time to learn about and discuss them. In the end, a night session was held on using standards in collective bargaining, in organizing self-employed rural workers, and in promoting women's rights. The workshop evaluation asked the ILO to provide more opportunities for workers to become acquainted with the labour standards relevant to them.[32]

The lesson that may be drawn from this is that labour and human rights standards and conventions are of direct relevance to workers all over the world, to their dignity and quality of life. Enormous gains have been won over the years by the labour movement – from limits on working hours to the right to freedom of association, from grievance procedures to minimum wage provisions. Many of these are formalized in the International Labour Code, which workers everywhere should both protect and strengthen. Protect, because there is a trend in some quarters to complain about 'over-regulation'; the reality, however, is under-regulation, because no standard anywhere has been totally and universally implemented. And strengthen, because universal implementation is a worthy target.

1. Tjänstemannens Centralorganisation (TCO), *Equality – A Question of Power: Women's Perspectives on Working Life and Welfare*, TCO, Stockholm, n.d.
2. The subject of discrimination on the basis of disability is addressed in *Women and Disability* by Esther Boylan in this series, Zed Books, London, 1991.
3. *Equality in Employment and Occupation: General Survey of the Reports on Convention No. 111*. Report of the Committee of Experts on the Application of Conventions and Recommendations, ILO, Geneva, 1988.
4. United Nations, *The Nairobi Forward-looking Strategies for the Advancement of Women*, United Nations Department of Public Information, New York, 1986.
5. International Confederation of Free Trade Unions (ICFTU), *Equality: the Continuing Challenge – Strategies for Success*. Report of the Fifth World Women's Conference, ICFTU, Brussels, 1991.
6. Ibid.
7. United Nations Development Programme (UNDP), *Human Development Report 1993*, UNDP, New York, 1993.
8. Vasudha Dhagamwar, *Education as a Tool of Ensuring Equality for Women in Employment*, Report to ILO Equality of Rights Branch, ILO, Geneva, n.d.
9. UNDP.
10. Unity A. Chari, *Positive Action Measures to Promote the Equality of Women in Employment in Zimbabwe*, ILO, Geneva, 1993.
11. Trades Union Congress, *More Than You Bargained For: a TUC Negotiator's Pack on Bargaining for Equality*, TUC, London, 1991.
12. TCO.
13. ILO, *Technical Background Paper for Tripartite Symposium on Equality of Opportunity and Treatment for Men and Women in Employment in Industrialised Countries*, ILO, Geneva, 1990.
14. Public Services International, *Paths to Power*. Background paper for Second World Women's Conference, PSI, Ferney-Voltaire, 1992.
15. Morley Gunderson, *Comparable Worth and Gender Discrimination: an International Perspective*, ILO, Geneva, 1993.
16. ILO, Technical Background Paper.
17. Jacy Corea Curado, 'Message from Brazil', in *News from IRENE*, No. 14, 1991, p. 30.
18. Itziar Lozano and Eleodora Contreras, 'Supporting women workers in FTZs in Latin America', in *News from IRENE*, No. 15/16, 1992, p. 29.
19. 'Women workers forced to fight hard all over the world for the right to maternity leave', in *Free Labour World*, March 1993.
20. ILO, *Workers with Family Responsibilities: General Survey of the Reports on Convention No. 156 and Recommendation No. 165*. Report to the Eightieth Session of the International Labour Conference, ILO, Geneva, 1993.
21. Ibid.
22. ILO, *Namibian Women and Employment: the Promotion of Equal Opportunities, Documents of a Tripartite Symposium*, ILO, Geneva, 1992.
23. 'Workers are parents too', in *Asian Women Workers' Newsletter*, Vol. 9, No. 4, 1990.
24. ILO, 'Women workers: protection or equality?', in *Conditions of Work Digest*, No. 2, 1987.
25. For further discussion of occupational health issues see *Women and Health* by Patricia Smyke in this series, Zed Books, London, 1991.
26. For further discussion of violence against women see *Women and Human Rights* by Katarina Tomaševski in this series, Zed Books, London, 1993.
27. Canadian Labour Congress, 'We can do it: end the violence against women'. Policy statement to 19th Constitutional Convention, June 1993.
28. 'Committee against Sexual Harassment', *Sauti ya Siti*, Tanzania Media Women's Association, No. 15, 1991.
29. 'Women and law', in *Tribune*, a women and development quarterly, International Women's Tribune Center, No. 45, 1990.
30. For further discussion of legal literacy see Tomaševski.
31. ILO Regional Office for Asia and the Pacific, *ILO Standards and Women Workers*, ILO, Bangkok, 1990.
32. 'Report of ILO workshop on the advancement of women in rural workers' organisations in Africa, May 1992', ILO, Geneva, 1992.

8 ORGANIZING FOR CHANGE

When we are isolated we are weak. How can there be a noise from a single hand? But if we form a group and then clap, a loud noise can be made.[1]

THE VITAL SPARK that is the human spirit seems very difficult – and, it is to be hoped, impossible – to extinguish. The *Human Development Report 1993* draws attention to the millions of people worldwide who are excluded from both economic and political participation, but also to the enormous upsurge in recent years in community action and people's organization.[2] Much of this has been led by women. The impact of grassroots action is twofold: in the process of organizing around an issue, women are strengthened. They learn about an issue and about their rights, and discover their own strengths and potential. At the same time, women move out of their 'invisible' or subordinate roles and make their voices heard.

COLLECTIVE ACTION ☐ Women organize around their own most pressing needs and priorities, deciding their own objectives and working out their own strategies. Women may organize around their reproductive role: lack of running water; a local schoolmaster's abuse of their daughters; rising food prices; or around their productive role: pooling savings to break free from the moneylender; forming a co-operative to market products more widely; uniting against exploitative wages or dangerous working conditions. A helpful distinction has been made between practical and strategic gender needs. Women's practical gender needs stem from their role in the existing division of labour: action addressing these needs focuses on making it easier for women to carry out their predominantly reproductive responsibilities. Women's strategic gender needs refer to the transformation of the division of labour itself: action addressing these needs affirms the rights of women, challenges the specific elements of their subordination, and works towards a better organization of society.[3] It should be emphasized that both are legitimate needs; the challenge is not to choose between them but to develop strategies that can respond in a comprehensive way to both.

Women organize into structures that can help them achieve their goals. As individuals their power and resources may be negligible, but together they become more than the sum of the parts: they become an organization that can both protect and support its members, and promote their interests. They may also gain the status to become eligible for services such as credit or training, to send representatives to bodies that affect their work, and to gain a voice in the political process. The forms of organization vary enormously – it is a question of finding the one that suits the outlook and experience of the women concerned while achieving their objectives. Development agencies could usefully explore the benefits of organizational support as well as the standard project-based activities. This would mean providing back-up for the efforts of women's groups to meet, mobilize, communicate and lobby.

A choice women sometimes face is whether to join existing organizations – from workers' associations to local community groups – or form their own. What has been noticeable over recent years is the way women have brought the two options closer: they have, for example, formed their own groupings within established organizations, and made links between these and women's movements outside.

They have strengthened many traditional organizations such as trade unions (see below) by bringing a new vision and practice of organizing to them.

PUTTING PRESSURE ON DECISION-
MAKERS □ In order to maximize the effect of local, grassroots actions, connections need to be made between them, and from them to the decision-makers. Women's actions and groupings, however informal, must not be viewed as marginal or irrelevant. The knowledge on which they are based and the priorities they establish must inform national and international policy-making. Who are the decision-makers? Both the politicians, those most susceptible to popular pressure, and the controllers of markets, susceptible to regulation by governments but also to action by the buying public.

The relationship between public policy and community action was explored at a seminar on women in extreme poverty organized by the United Nations Division for the Advancement of Women (DAW). Community action may collaborate with the state, assisting with the delivery of, say, public health or literacy, or it may be adversarial, by focusing attention on the inadequacy of policies to alleviate poverty.[4] Both collaborative and adversarial activities have their place, and a creative tension should exist between them; but the adversarial element is crucial in keeping up the pressure for change, in making the state accountable, and in shifting the balance of power in favour of the poor. Diane Elson argues thus:

**[The] legitimate role and vital
contribution of activist groups is to ...
inform, pressurise, mobilise, criticise,
and campaign so that both private and
public sector agents are given
incentives to respond in ways that
extend the entitlements of poor**

**women. They are ... catalysts, with the potential
to trigger reactions much more powerful than
their own size and resources would suggest and
to generate a process of genuinely 'public'
rather than merely 'state' policy.[5]**

In India, the Self-Employed Women's Association (SEWA) has also found that action of many kinds is needed:

**SEWA has found that in order to be effective,
struggle has to be carried out at all levels of
injustice. First through direct action – meeting
with the employers or police, and [holding]
marches, demonstrations and strikes. ... Second,
[we] deal with government departments through
complaints and use the legal structure by filing
cases in court. Finally, SEWA tries to bring about
policy changes ... by campaigns, workshops,
studies and advocacy. But basic to all these
strategies is the need to organise the workers.[6]**

ORGANIZING IN NETWORKS □ Net-
working is a strategy particularly well-suited to the desire of many women's associations for exchange and mutual support without the formality of bureaucratic and hierarchical structures. Women's recognition of the power of collective strength has resulted in the formation of networks of many different sorts, local and international, grouped around one issue or open and wide-ranging. Some of the women involved in *Rede Mulher* (the Women's Network) in Brazil describe how they see networking: 'We may draw an analogy to fishing lines. Used separately, each line can catch only one fish at a time. But when the individual lines are joined into a net the total capacity is geometrically increased ... [also] in a fishing net there is no hierarchy among the knots. Any tear may be individually repaired without jeopardizing the whole.'[7] The benefits of networking include exchanging information and experience; maximizing the impact of local actions; and breaking down barriers

that appear to separate women in different situations.

Development Alternatives with Women for a New Era (DAWN) is a think-tank and action network started by Third World women, based on regional subgroups with global links. One of its priority areas has been the effects of debt and structural adjustment, and a current project is to develop 'alternative economic frameworks'. Organizing around global investment and the international division of labour, with special attention to women workers, are Women Working Worldwide (see below) and the International Restructuring Education Network Europe (IRENE). Women's World Banking was set up in 1979 to help women gain access to credit in order to start their own businesses; to set up national support organizations; and to establish a global support network for banking and business women to exchange ideas and techniques.

Regional networks play an important role at an intermediate stage between local and global action. One of the earliest organizations to take up issues of concern to women in Africa was the Association of African Women for Research and Development (AAWORD). Other regional networks include the Caribbean Association for Feminist Research and Action (CAFRA), which works closely with women in trade unions, and the Committee for Asian Women (CAW), which focuses on women industrial workers. (See also the resource list in Annex III.)

The recent evolution of more or less unstructured alliances should not be seen as the first or only form of networking. Since the early twentieth century women have formed associations around a common experience or concern, and many of them are now well-established national and international federations. A few examples are Soroptomists International, the International Federation of Business and Professional Women, the International Council of Jewish Women, Zonta International. They identify their particular strength as the fact that they consist of autonomous groups engaged in local action which, by making common cause on certain issues, can exert considerable pressure on governments and inter-government bodies. More recently, women in a number of developing countries have been exploring the benefits of professional associations and networks both to support the position of existing women in a sector or occupation, and to encourage the entry into it of more women. These might be women entrepreneurs, for example, or women in technical and scientific occupations. The Women for Women Foundation (Asia) is an association of and for women managers, which provides research, training and counselling services as well as more informal means of support. For more information on women's networks, see *Women and Empowerment: Participation and Decision-Making* in this series.

ORGANIZING IN CO-OPERATIVES ☐

The development of co-operatives has often taken place where no other form of organization existed. While formal co-operatives are generally legally registered bodies, women have also formed many sorts of looser groupings – sometimes called 'pre-cooperatives' – to help them save, for example, or market their products. Providing the means for women to turn these small-scale and *ad hoc* groupings into full co-operatives, and to maximize the benefits of co-operative membership, is one approach to the promotion of equal opportunities and development through organization.

Over the past two decades the co-operative movement generally has been growing in size and importance. Women's participation has increased significantly, 'generating renewed vitality and growth', according to the ILO.[8] Although co-operatives vary enormously in the scale and nature of their activities, basically they are associations set up to achieve economic and social benefits for their members through and as a group. Key characteristics are democratic control and the equitable distribution of both costs and benefits; these and other principles are set out in the ILO's Co-operatives (Developing Countries) Recommendation, 1966 (No. 127). Co-operatives are set up for many different purposes, but may be grouped in two broad categories: production or workers' co-operatives, where the members work together, and service co-operatives, the most common type, which include marketing, consumer, and credit groups. They may provide a range of services for their members. Co-operatives are found in all countries and involve over 500 million people worldwide; in some countries the co-operative sector is the largest economic institution.[9]

A PLACE FOR WOMEN? Many women, deprived of control over their labour, and exploited by middlemen, have an enormous amount to gain from the co-operative system. The Nairobi Forward-looking Strategies for the Advancement of Women identify co-operatives as an important means of improving women's living and working conditions and promoting their participation in development. Anila Dholakia spells out the benefits of co-operatives in creating employment, increasing women's income-generating assets and capacities, and improving their social status:

Women can make use of the co-operative movement as a tool for gaining greater access to a range of resources and services ... and obtain a platform from which to make the voice of labouring women heard more effectively.[10]

Areas that have proved especially fruitful for women's co-operative activity include traditional and modern handicraft production, and the processing and sale of foodstuffs. Women's participation is highest however, in savings and credit co-operatives. More than half the members of these types of association are women, and their participation in management is higher than in other types. One example is the Lesotho Co-operative Credit Union League, which has 22,000 members, 75 per cent of them women.

Nevertheless, women have been excluded from, or disadvantaged in, many areas of co-operative activity. One major example is their exclusion from most agricultural co-operatives – which require members to own land – in spite of women's key role in agricultural production. Other co-operatives restrict membership to the (male) head of the household, or refuse to acknowledge the rights of women over the crops, milk or handicrafts they have produced. This exclusion doubly disadvantages women because many government-subsidized inputs, as well as access to the most extensive marketing services, are made available through co-operatives. Such policies and practices, which may be underpinned by national or local laws, are also reinforced by factors such as women's heavy workload, restricted education, and lack of confidence. Where women make up part of the membership, even a substantial part, men tend to be in positions of authority as managers or members of the governing committee.

WOMEN'S CO-OPERATIVES A weakness of co-operative development aimed specifically at women has been the tendency for it to take the form of isolated projects, marginal to wider social and economic processes. Women-only schemes have tended to concentrate on traditional female activities and have often received less

Acquiring skills and experience through co-operatives: carpet weavers in Afghanistan

funding, credit and training than general schemes.[11] It has occasionally happened that particularly successful projects have been taken over by men, an appropriation made possible by statutes that failed to define or limit membership.

Nevertheless, there are many gains to be made in women's co-operatives, not least the acquisition of skills and experience that will enable women to participate actively in mixed co-operatives and other spheres of economic, social and political activity. The ILO's programme to promote and support co-operatives is one of its most important areas of technical assistance. Assistance to women's groups – pre-co-operatives and formal co-operatives – has increased, and activities addressing women's specific needs have been developed based on the findings of a substantial study carried out in the early 1980s.[12] A further major study was carried out in six Asian countries in 1988 and 1989.[13] The programme pro-

vides advisory services on co-operative legislation and ongoing research, documentation and information. Skills training is also recognized as being particularly necessary to enable women to start up, or participate actively in, a co-operative association. Training activities include business management, organizational and communications skills, as well as basic co-operative education. Increasingly, parallel provision is being made to reduce women's workload. The impact of a series of regional conferences and seminars in Africa has been felt in a number of ways, including the establishment of a women's section in the Co-operative College of Tanzania.

MAKING CO-OPERATIVES WORK Three particular obstacles in the way of women's initiatives in production are the lack of credit, the exploitative role of agents, and poor marketing. Co-operatives can help

EXPERIENCE FROM RWANDA
Gabriella Nimbona provides training and support for women's co-operatives in Rwanda. Her assessment of their benefits includes the following points: 'Women's co-ops offer an effective channel for diffusing new ideas, because in groups they are easier to reach and mobilise than as individuals. [They] give women access to a wider social reality and a taste of business activity, so that they can help each other by providing both social and economic support. Women co-op members dare to take risks. ... Individual problems are solved together ... those who know teach the others.'[14]

overcome all three, through the pooling of resources, providing opportunities for training, and strengthening women's bargaining power. Public policy and technical assistance can support them by:

● encouraging women's membership;

● improving their technical and managerial skills;

● providing co-operative education and improving advisory services;

● ensuring equality in national co-operative legislation.

ORGANIZING IN THE RURAL SECTOR

□ The very nature and conditions of rural employment – its scattered workplaces, combination of own-account and waged employment, traditional systems and power structures, lower levels of education and literacy, and, often, the pressure simply to survive – mean that it is the hardest and last sector to organize. As the ILO says:

Poverty combining material want and undignified conditions of labour is closely related to the absence of a workers' organisation or a co-operative to protect and further the interests of rural workers. Large

numbers of the rural poor ... have no such organisation to turn to. The few that exist are frequently too weak to adequately represent and assist their members.[15]

The benefits of organizing are becoming more widely recognized in a number of spheres, including income generation and the provision of agricultural extension services. The key difference is that women are not simply brought together in a group to carry out a preconceived activity or receive training, but are helped to mobilize around their priorities, run their own activities, and develop and use their group strength to achieve objectives they have defined.

A number of countries are sponsoring the formation of women's groups in order to improve women's access to extension services. In Indonesia, for example, more than 3,500 women's groups have been set up as part of the farmer extension system. India is piloting schemes using female 'information brokers' to organize women into groups that will hold regular meetings with the extension officers.[16]

SELF-HELP AND INFORMAL ORGANIZING Women have responded to the lack of rural organizations, and to their exclusion from resources and services, by organizing in less structured and formal ways. It is nothing new for women to pool their resources in order to make their lives a little easier, or to increase their influence or bargaining power. Women's work parties are common in many rural areas, and help women farmers cope with peak labour demands or especially hard and time-consuming jobs such as land preparation. The work parties have also been used as a platform for bargaining with employers or to help women gain access to productive resources, such as credit and technology. Informal groupings, established for a common interest, can thus provide a base for formal organization and develop into pressure groups for change.

A study by Barbara Thomas on household strategies in Kenya showed that the functions of most women's groups are in response to their marginalization by commercial processes. She identified three different types of group in Murang'a District in Central Province: associations for income-generating activities; revolving loan funds; and groups that focus on exchange activities.[17] A number are active in all three areas, with great flexibility in adjusting to the needs of their members. Some associations undertake community development projects as well. Membership of the groups also provides a network for information-sharing, and a means of communicating with the local administration and extension services.

Ways to encourage the linking of women may include facilitating the organization of discussion forums and meetings to assess problems, identify or create the means to overcome them, and agree priorities. For example: women's access to the market in the local town may be restricted by several factors: lack of transport; lack of child care; lack of market information; lack of demand; and lack of time because of their many other jobs. A possible solution agreed by a group may be to take collective action. A formal or informal co-operative could arrange a sharing of the tasks: one or two women to look after the children, and perhaps prepare some food, while the others go to market. The group as a whole may pay for the transport of those who go. At the market they may share a stand, or offer each other support in other ways, in order to strengthen their position.

STRENGTHENING RURAL WORKERS' ORGANIZATIONS

Rural trade unions can fulfil a range of functions, from improving workers' living and working conditions to income generation and employment cre-

SELF-HELP IN SIERRA LEONE

The Kassassi Women's Agricultural Development Association (KWADA) started in 1976 as a small-scale initiative by a group of village women in a poor and isolated area of Sierra Leone. The main occupation of the village is subsistence farming, and many young people have left for the towns. In an effort to create opportunities for their children, and to increase their farming revenue, a group of women looked at the potential of a nearby area of communal swampland. They joined forces to drain and clear it, dividing about 80 acres into individual farms to provide food for their families. Another 20 acres is farmed communally on a rota basis, growing rice, groundnuts and cassava. This communal land is seen as central to the members' livelihood. The sale of the first harvest provided funds for second and subsequent cultivations. Now the produce is communally owned and sold at a fair price to members in the 'lean season' when no crops grow.

Although the association is run by women, it includes the whole community in its projects, in particular girls and boys who can earn money to pay their school fees by working on the farms. For the women involved, the benefits are not purely economic. 'Women are more vocal, and consider themselves as part and parcel of society, getting involved in the decision-making of the village.' This is the observation of Sally Formah-Kamara, who has helped the project expand thanks to a solidarity fund set up by the 1% Women Worldwide Campaign of Scottish Education and Action for Development (SEAD).[18]

PHOTO: ILO/J. MAILLARD

Meeting at a rural women's centre in Zimbabwe

ation. One of the most potentially effective ways of empowering women is to enable and encourage their participation in rural workers' organizations.

IFPAAW, the international trade secretariat for agricultural and plantation workers, is co-ordinating a wide-ranging project on behalf of the ILO, financed by Danish and Norwegian development aid. The project aims to help rural workers develop and manage their own trade unions and related organizations, thus strengthening their position in relation to landlords and employers. The objective is to achieve this primarily through promoting the participation of women, thus also strengthening their position at work and in the union. The principal strategy is to train a corps of women activists in rural workers' organizations and a cadre of women specialists who can support their work. The project operates in three Asian and three African countries, and has been extended for a further

period due to its success. A separate project with similar objectives is being carried out in Central America.

Workers' education with an active learning approach provides the basis for the programme. Topics include appropriate technology and inheritance laws, as well as labour standards, organization building, and financial management. The methodology has been experimental as well as participatory, one important strand being the use of drama. Women are identified by IFPAAW affiliates as suitable for training as resource-persons/organizers, following which they go back to their organizations to run grassroots seminars and mobilizing activities. The project has succeeded in putting in place an aware and committed cadre of women in dozens of workers' organizations. It should be stressed that most are rank-and-file members with the same background and education as the women they work with. Through changes in the women's own attitudes and outlook, and changes in the attitudes and structures of the organizations involved, the project has also resulted in more women gaining positions of responsibility. At the same time the organizations themselves have become stronger and more active in representing the interests of rural workers, male and female.[19]

ORGANIZING IN THE INFORMAL SECTOR □

Although the informal sector is defined as 'unorganized', and own-account activities predominate, it would be wrong to assume that no forms of organization exist among self-employed, marginalized, or unemployed workers. Various self-help and solidarity mechanisms exist, at the personal level and in neighbourhoods and occupational groups. These include, for example, groups of traders or self-employed persons set up to negotiate with municipal officials, protect themselves against competition, or share a potential market. Some are longstanding mutual aid societies, such as revolving credit societies and cooperative-type groupings. Some are newer groups with more strategic objectives, called by the International Confederation of Free Trade Unions (ICFTU) 'crisis trade unionism, or poverty unionism, a manifestation of the growing problems of high employment and low income'.[20]

NEW FORMS OF ORGANIZATION What is remarkable is that in spite of fragmented workplaces, the absence of the 'normal' conditions for organizing, and the enormous pressures on them to manage, women from traditionally unorganized sectors – from the self-employed to domestic servants – are setting up their own associations and unions, and developing new forms of organization in the process. These range from education centres to co-operatives, from neighbourhood

to workers' associations. The South African Domestic Workers' Union (SADWU) and the Union of Women Domestic Employees in Brazil are among a number of organizations that are now well-established, in spite of the difficulty of mobilizing a workforce that is not only scattered but that may not always be recognized as 'real' workers. Another development has been the community unions in Japan, which organize workers left out by the other unions, including migrant workers, part-timers, homeworkers, temporary workers and the unemployed. They are locally based rather than centred on industries and sectors, and number more women than men among the organizers as well as among the members.[21]

Recognizing the importance of initiatives such as these, the ILO is undertaking a programme to look into the how and the why of them. With respect to domestic servants, studies are going on in some Latin American countries and will probably be carried out in one or two industrialized countries as well. Other studies will include self-employed activities such as trading (West Africa) and knitting (Italy), and women workers in free trade zones and in the rural sector. The objective is to develop strategies for encouraging women in unorganized activities to join trade unions.

India provides a number of models in terms of successful structures, and repeated examples of women in the poorest and most oppressed circumstances finding strength and confidence through collective action. Organizations such as SEWA and the Working Women's Forum never lose sight of the fact that their members are desperately poor, but they link income-raising with action to enhance the bargaining power, status and self-confidence of their members.

THE WORKING WOMEN'S FORUM The Working Women's Forum (WWF) is based in South India and is made up of some of the poorest workers in the informal sector, both urban and rural. It started in 1978, and now has 200,000 members in four states. They pursue over 100 different occupations from incense-making to handicrafts, from fishing to agricultural labouring. The major programmes are credit assistance; training and awareness-raising; employment and support services; and health and family welfare. The WWF also plays an active lobbying role, both nationally and internationally. Its key organizing characteristic is leadership from below: not only the members but the great majority of staff and leaders are poor, working-class women, who establish priorities based on the needs of the very poor and run the WWF through a decentralized system of self-management. Much may be learnt from the WWF's methods and structure.

The unique nature of this movement ... is solely due to the participation of poor women.... WWF is a movement of women which believes that the leadership should come from the poor, if the poor are to come out of the 'poverty trap'. Thus, for a change, the elites must learn from the poor women too. For example, the planning process in WWF is always a 'bottom–up' process and not a 'trickle-down' – this process has been described as a 'counter-culture by poor women'.[22]

The WWF came into being in response to poor women's need for credit. At first it tried to help women deal with the national banks, but bureaucracy and prejudice proved too entrenched. The women therefore set up a banking system of their own, the Working Women's Co-operative Society (WWCS). Apart from credit provision, the WWF also helps members improve their economic position through bulk buying of raw materials, skills training, and market development. Members are orga-

nized in self-managed groups of ten or so women. Each elects a group leader, who collects the payments and accepts sole responsibility for the repayment of all the loans in the group; in return, she has a larger loan. The next level in the WWF, area organizers, are mostly recruited from among the group leaders, and so the leadership is built up from within the membership. The WWF stresses that the loan groups are not simply economic units; groups in the same area come together and become a 'social force', taking up the issues confronting poor women.[23]

The WWF also provides education and training outside the WWCS, especially in organizational and mobilization techniques, and communication skills. It helps women in different occupational and trade groups by bringing them together to identify issues and grievances (for example, piece-rate levels) and supports their mass meetings and representations to policymakers. The WWF has created the National Union of Working Women in order to pursue some of its most specifically organizational work on behalf of women's pay and conditions of employment. One example is the campaign on behalf of the lace-makers of Narsapur:

A WWF VICTORY
The lace industry in the Andhra Pradesh town of Narsapur was controlled for many years by exporters who, through a hierarchy of middlemen, paid the lowest of low rates to women artisans working long hours under poor conditions, mostly in their homes. To break the hold of the exporters the WWF helped the women organize in groups, and provided loans to increase their opportunities for self-employment. Over a period of four years 8,000 artisans were organized, and a producers' co-operative was set up with over 4,000 shareholders. The ILO helped the WWF to set up an export system, and the Government of India provided the co-operative with orders. At the same time, the exporters have been forced to put up the rates they pay.[24]

PHOTO: ILO/J. MAILLARD

Labor Day demonstration, USA

In *A Profile of Empowerment*, a video about the work of the WWF, Jaya Arunachalam, founder member and president, says that the organization has two main goals for the future. The first is to increase the political pressure: on the one hand by organizing more demonstrations, petitions, and lobbies, reinforcing the strength and high profile of the movement, and on the other hand through its growing network of contacts and advocates at state, national and international level. The second is to extend the reach of the WWF to more women, but not simply by expanding it, and certainly not by attempting to make it nationwide. The wish of the WWF is that other groups and movements will reproduce what they are doing, take from their experience what might be useful, adapt it to their needs, and so share with other poor women the benefits clearly gained by those in the WWF.

ORGANIZING IN THE FORMAL SECTOR □ Women in the formal sector have organized on workplace issues in two main ways: within the mainstream trade unions (see below) and in their own associations. Often they have no choice but to use their own organizations: where formal trade unions do not exist, or are barred from entering export zones and factories, or lack the experience or motivation to organize women in non-standard occupations. The Grassroots Women Workers' Centre in Taiwan and the Korean Women Workers' Association both came into being in order to give women the space to organize separately. Recognizing the need to connect with the labour movement, however, their objectives also include putting pressure on the mainstream unions to reform their structures and practices.

WOMEN WORKERS' ASSOCIATIONS
Obliged to draw on their own resources,

women workers have found new ways of organizing, based on their particular circumstances and needs. Various forms of passive resistance have been used, as well as direct struggles for better conditions. What has been found again and again is that when women have the chance to meet, both at and outside the workplace, conditions are created for the development of awareness leading to group action. The balance of power is, of course, weighted heavily against them; however, women have found enormous strength, and have achieved real victories against the odds, as they unite with women not just in other local factories, but in other countries.

In 1982, the first 'sympathy' strike took place in the Bataan EPZ (Export Processing Zone) in the Philippines, a zone-wide stoppage by workers, irrespective of their employer. 200 workers walked out of their factory in protest against forced overtime. As they were attacked by the zone police the word spread to other factories, and 20,000 women from 23 factories also stopped work in sympathy and solidarity. One consequence was the granting of concessions by a worried management but, more important, the strike led to the formation of the Bataan Alliance of Labour Association (AMB-A-BALA) with the aim of maintaining solidarity and co-ordinating union activity in the zone.[25]

INTERNATIONAL SOLIDARITY The
export processing zones and industries have not only provided the conditions for women to organize locally; because of their global links through foreign capital, they have also provided an international perspective. Women in other countries – fellow workers as well as consumers of their products – have also come to see the long and complex chain which binds them. New technology, while internationalizing the production process, also provides the means for women to exchange their experiences and offer each other solidarity. Women from the same industry in different countries, and activists, have met or communicated to give each other support, share information and develop strategies.

A conference on women and the international division of labour, held in London in 1983, analysed the role of TNCs in creating 'unstable and vulnerable patterns of employment, be it in Malaysia or Scotland'.[26] This conference led to the establishment of the network Women Working Worldwide, which aims to support the struggles of women as workers globally. The Manchester group has produced an education package and exhibition as part of a campaign on clothing and textiles called *The Labour behind the Label*. The London group focuses on electronics, and has produced *Common Interests: Women Organising in Global Electronics*, a book based on the organizing experiences of women in thirteen countries worldwide.

WOMEN IN TRADE UNIONS Trade
unions are forces for social and political change with an influence out of proportion to their numbers. This is one reason why the participation of women in unions is of particular importance. One of the most interesting developments in recent years has been the way in which women's entry has brought about changes in attitudes and structures, and helped unions make alliances with other groups – from women's movements to environmental lobbyists and campaigners on debt – in order to work more effectively for development and social justice. The principle that all workers have the right to organize freely forms the basis of one of the most fundamental of ILO instruments, Convention No. 87: Freedom of Association and Protection of the Right to Organise (1948).

TRADE UNIONS IN DEVELOPMENT
The former deputy director-general of the ILO, Bertil Bolin, is emphatic about the importance of union organization: 'Trade unions are among the most effective channels for social and economic participation of men and women workers. ... This is particularly true in the many countries where trade unions are the only representative bodies of workers, who would otherwise lack effective means of achieving their aspirations and promoting their welfare. In the absence of other channels for presenting their claims, or of instruments of social and political action, workers are steadily expanding the role of trade unions beyond the traditional function of collective bargaining. ... Very often they are involved in ... running welfare programmes and self-help schemes, community development projects, literacy and vocational training courses, small workers' enterprises, savings and loans associations, health and family centres, and a whole host of other activities which go beyond the conventional realm of trade union action, but which in many cases they alone have the capacity to perform on behalf of workers.[27]

With the full participation of women, the potential for trade unions to act as agents of social transformation is much more likely to be realized. Over the years many unions have come to reflect society rather than seek to change it, and nowhere is this more obvious than in the lack of representation of women in their decision-making processes. Valerie Ellis, deputy general secretary of the British trade union for professionals, managers and specialists IPMS, points out that 'those with more power in the market place or job hierarchy tend to be those with power in unions'.[28]

The gender bias in unions has been compounded by their indifference to the plight of low-paid, casual, seasonal, temporary and informal workers, of whom most are women. It is both recent and by no means universal that unions have come to see that if their traditional structures and forms of organizing do not respond to the needs of these workers, the structures should change rather than the workers be excluded. Unions have to make room for 'women's culture'.[29] As Amanda Villatora of the El Salvador national union centre, Central de Trabajadores Democràticos (CTD) has stated:

Equality must begin within the union. The trade union must encourage, must disseminate information, but also must prepare, must educate and train women, and must give them ... self-esteem.[30]

BARRIERS TO THE PARTICIPATION OF WOMEN

The obstacles to women's participation in unions are extensions of the obstacles they face on the labour market:

- Women's domestic responsibilities already represent a second shift on top of the working day, so union meetings and activities make a third shift.

- The sectors and occupations where most women work are often the least organized anyway, and their part-time and temporary work contracts have also made them more difficult to reach.

- The structures and policies of the union, venues and times of meetings, and lack of women in authority are likely to favour men's priorities and working patterns, and marginalize, disfavour or put off women. 'We'll show a real interest in unions when they show a real interest in us,' said a Mexicana assembly line worker in California.[31]

- There may be outright hostility from fathers and husbands, employers, and male trade unionists to the participation of women.

A woman member of an electronics union in the USA's Silicon Valley tells of her experience:

The first time we showed up at the meeting, we were a little bit nervous, so we ... all sat together at the back. Some of the guys got all upset and grumbled that the ''cunt block'' was taking over. Well, that broke down all the confidence we had built up in two of the girls ... and they left. ... Some of the guys have been real supportive ... but a lot of them think we're ''pinking-up'' their turf. What do they think we're going to do, put up lace curtains? This is a union, not a boys' club.[32]

WOMEN BREAK THROUGH For a long time the concerns of women, and their ways of dealing with them, were seen as evidence that women were not 'proper' workers and trade unionists and that they did not understand the 'real' issues or how to organize to achieve them. The biggest breakthrough of recent years – still only partial – has been the recognition that women's issues and methods are not just valid, but may offer greater possibilities for real change to the benefit of men and women, families and workers. Conversely, women are engaging more directly with 'mainstream' issues, recognizing that every issue is a women's issue.

The breakthrough has taken place because of the build-up of numbers of women, the concerted efforts of many activists, and the path-breaking of a small number of women leaders. Women's trade union membership is holding steady or increasing at a time when male participation is declining, though differences between occupations are substantial. The main regional exception is central and eastern Europe where women's rapidly rising unemployment is having a direct impact on their participation in unions. The International Confederation of Free Trade Unions (ICFTU) reports that 34 per cent of its membership worldwide is female; and women have made the most of their numbers by linking up within and across unions through women's committees, caucuses, and coalitions. Over 90 per cent of ICFTU affiliates replying to a questionnaire in 1991 reported having a special structure and/or officer responsible for women's and equality questions. Even more important, in a growing number of cases (some 50 per cent) the women's committee reports directly to the highest decision-making body on its activities and policies.[33] While much remains to be done, the conditions for change do now exist.

TRADE UNION TRAINING As more women joined trade unions, it became clear that there were barriers to their participation in educational activities, from the overt favouring of men to women's more limited availability. Educators stress the need for positive action measures to be applied to general training: invitations should specify that attendance by women is expected, on the basis of their numbers in the membership, for example, or one man and one woman from each participating branch or union. Careful consideration should also be given to the timing and venue of training sessions and to support services such as child care. A gender-aware approach to all training, not just women's training, should be encouraged, and equality issues should be woven in, whatever the subject: negotiators are increasingly being trained to bargain for pay and employment equity, for example.

There is also a need for women to have the opportunity to deal separately with certain issues of special concern, as well as to develop the tools and confidence to play a fuller role in mainstream activities. The benefits of special programmes for women have been found to be enormously positive. Women's training is now widespread in most unions in industrialized countries and covers a range of topics: as well as

A momentum has been created... The long road to equality

basic trade unionism and general equality seminars, unions may offer specialized training for equal opportunities officers and women educators; assertiveness and leadership training; and special training opportunities for women stuck in low-paid and 'dead-end' jobs. Systematic training for women members in developing countries has been relatively recent, but it has proved a breakthrough in terms of skills development, consciousness-raising, and the blossoming of self-confidence. Not only has women's participation in unions increased, but they have also gained skills which have improved their job opportunities.

INTERNATIONAL ACTION Trade unions are often part of regional and international networks that can strengthen the links between workers and maximize their influence. Unions in the same sector – transport, for example, or the food industry – can become part of international trade secretariats. The International Confederation of Free Trade Unions (ICFTU) is one of three worldwide federations of national union centres. The ICFTU's policy on women's equality has become noticeably more proactive, especially since its very successful World Women's Conference in 1991. After 'encouraging' women's participation for a number of years, the organization has adopted a Positive Action Programme which will:

- set up a Task Force to plan and monitor activities;

- raise special funding for the programme;

- establish quotas for attendance at sponsored activities;

- systematically introduce a gender perspective into all research, training and technical co-operation activities;

- organize women-specific programmes where needed;

- make regular reports and evaluations of all activities.

FINAL CONCLUSION ☐ The conclusion of this book, and of many men and women, is that the world cannot afford to do without women's full contribution at every level of social, economic and political activity. The empowerment of women is an end in itself, because it is a question of basic human rights. It is also a means to an end: the transformation of social structures so that they serve the needs of people rather than ignoring, suppressing or distorting them. Development would return to a biological or commonsense definition: the unfolding of the potential of individuals and communities. Work would be organized in a way that enhanced rather than diminished the quality of life of those who labour.

The preceding chapters have looked at the many facets of women's work, and the significant increase of women's participation in many forms of economic activity. What has been the impact? It is a question to which there is no final answer, because change continues all the time. Not all change is positive, and we need to be vigilant. The power of the status quo is great, and there are parts of the world and sectors of work where little progress can be seen in the lives of working women. What is more, we must face up to attempts on several fronts to put the clock back: efforts to lower labour standards, reduce social benefits and cut back services are having a negative impact on many women. Many other women are being threatened by a return to values and beliefs that promote the subordination of women: in different ways women's rights and autonomy are being threatened by a resurgence of Confucianism in China, and a hardening of Muslim, Hindu and Christian (both Roman Catholic and Protestant) fundamentalism. But let us look at the other side of the picture: in spite of the fact that poverty forces many women to work, and in spite of the poor conditions under which they work, the impact of millions of women coming into the labour force – as farmers, secretaries, teachers, bus drivers, traders, doctors – has been overwhelmingly positive. Women have shown what they can do, and it is becoming more and more difficult to confine them to the home, or to certain occupations, as their 'rightful' place. Women are sustaining households all over the world, and cannot be ignored or marginalized. The immense economic contribution of women is being recognized, as well as their social role. Women are gaining confidence and self-esteem, and are increasing their control over their lives.

Through workplace and other groupings, women are becoming stronger and more powerful. Over and above all this, women are showing that other targets, other forms of social and economic organization, other ways to development are possible and, indeed, desirable. Giving equal value to women's outlook and experience, to the reproductive as to the productive role, offers possibilities of a more holistic and human-centred approach to the structuring and development of societies. While it is impossible to see the final outcome, and the struggle is far from over, we must believe that an awareness has been created and a momentum built up that cannot be reversed.

1. WWF/UNICEF, *A Profile of Empowerment*, video on the Working Women's Forum.
2. United Nations Development Programme (UNDP), *Human Development Report 1993*, UNDP, New York, 1993.
3. See, for example, Caroline Moser, 'Gender planning in the Third World: meeting practical and strategic gender needs', in *World Development*, Vol. 17, No. 11, 1989.
4. J. Dreze and A. Sen, *Hunger and Public Action*, quoted in Diane Elson, 'Public action, poverty and development: a gender aware analysis', paper for seminar on Women in Extreme Poverty, UN Division for the Advancement of Women, Vienna, 1992, p. 10.
5. Elson, p. 18.
6. *SEWA in 1988*, Self Employed Women's Association, Ahmadabad, 1988, p. 20.
7. Moema Viezzer, 'Workshop on popular education with women', in Rachael Kamel (ed.), *Growing Together: Women, Feminism and Popular Education*, ISIS International and CEAAL, Rome/Santiago, 1988.
8. ILO, 'Women's participation in co-operatives', in *Women at Work*, No. 1, 1987, p. 1.
9. Ibid.
10. Ibid., pp. 8–9.
11. Linda Mayoux (ed.), *All Are Not Equal: African Women in Cooperatives*, Institute for African Alternatives, London, 1988.
12. ILO, 'Women's participation in co-operatives'.
13. D. Mavrogiannis, *Women's Involvement in Thrift and Credit Co-operatives in Selected Asian countries*, ILO, Geneva, 1991.
14. Gabriella Nimbona, 'Work with women's co-ops in Rwanda', GADU Newspack No. 14, Oxfam, Oxford, 1991.
15. ILO Advisory Committee on Rural Development, *Review of ILO Rural Development Activities since 1983*, ILO, Geneva, 1990.
16. United Nations Food and Agricultural Organization (FAO), *Women, Food Systems, and Agriculture*, FAO, Rome, 1990, p. 24.
17. Barbara Thomas, *Household Strategies for Adaptation and Change, Participation in Kenyan Rural Women's Associations* Working Paper No. 165, Michigan State University, 1988.
18. Scottish Education and Action for Development (SEAD), *Shoulder to Shoulder: a Teaching Pack on Women Organising Worldwide*, SEAD, Edinburgh, 1992.
19. Project documents and case studies from ILO Workers' Education Programme.
20. International Confederation of Free Trade Unions (ICFTU), *The Informal Sector and the Trade Union Movement in Latin America and the Caribbean: an Analysis and Proposals for Action*, ICFTU, Brussels, 1989, p. 11.
21. *News from IRENE*, No. 14, 1991.
22. Robert Chambers, *The Working Women's Forum: a Counter-culture by Poor Women*, UNICEF Regional Office for South Asia, New Delhi, 1985.
23. Working Women's Forum (India), reports, informational literature and video.
24. ILO, *Women at Work*, No. 2, 1986, p. 43.
25. Swasti Mitter, *Common Fate, Common Bond: Women in the Global Economy*, Pluto Press, London, 1986.
26. Ibid., p. 146.
27. Bertil Bolin, 'Key role of trade unions in promoting equality', in *Women at Work*, No. 1, 1988, p. 2.
28. PSI, Report of European Region Women's Seminar, Berlin, 1990.
29. Susan Eaton, *Women Workers, Unions and Industrial Sectors in North America*, ILO, Geneva, 1992.
30. Quoted in ICFTU, *Equality: the Continuing Challenge*, ICFTU, Brussels, 1991, p. 53.
31. Geraldine Reardon, *Common Interests: Women Organising in Global Electronics*, Women Working Worldwide, London, 1991, p. 37.
32. Ibid., p. 43.
33. ICFTU, *Equality: the Continuing Challenge*.

ANNEX I

DEFINITIONS

OF KEY TERMS

ACP African, Caribbean and Pacific countries: 69 former colonies which have special trade relations with the European Community through the Lome Convention.

adjustment responding to imbalances in national economies – often involving structural changes, hence structural adjustment policies and programmes.

balance of payments a country's revenues (including capital assets, investment and debts) set against expenditure for a given period .

conditionality obligations, such as adjustment measures and institutional reform, taken on by countries as part of aid or loan packages.

GDP gross domestic product, representing the value of goods and services produced by the state in a year.

GNP gross national product, the value of goods and services produced domestically, plus income earned by the state through overseas operations.

IBRD International Bank for Reconstruction and Development, generally known as the World Bank. Founded at the end of the Second World War; first aimed to help rebuild economies damaged by the war, later to provide funds for developing countries.

IFAT International Federation of Alternative Trade, co-ordinating the activities of alternative trading organizations worldwide.

IMF International Monetary Fund, resulting from the same initiative which produced the IBRD and GATT (see Chapter 5); still works closely with the World Bank. Intended to regulate and stabilize the international financial system.

NIC newly industrialized country.

NIEO new international economic order – the long-term objective of the group of 77 (now 96) developing countries which helped establish UNCTAD.

OECD Organisation for Economic Cooperation and Development: members are the world's industrialized nations.

over-represented a higher proportion than might be expected – if women are over-represented in a certain occupation, for example, the proportion of women is higher than in the workforce generally.

plant factory, including land, building, fixtures and machinery.

precarious· non-standard forms of employment such as casual and temporary work, which are inherently insecure.

primary commodities unprocessed goods , raw materials, mainly agricultural products and minerals, produced and exported by developing countries.

productivity quantity of goods and services put out per worker or workplace over a certain period.

terms of trade relationship between the price of exports and the cost of imports – worsening terms of trade mean that imports are costing more and/or exports earning less.

ANNEX II

A GUIDE TO EDUCATION AND ACTION

THIS ANNEX IS INTENDED to help readers make use of the book as the basis for study and action. All the ideas are suggestions or examples, not blueprints, taken from many sources. They should be adapted to the needs, circumstances and objectives of different groups. Some issues raised may help in the planning of projects – discussing some of the points about credit, training, or co-operatives in the light of your own experience may help develop a strategy for a production or marketing project. Other issues may suggest discussion topics for information and education programmes.

PLANNING A PROJECT

A project means an activity with a specific aim and limited timeframe. It might be quite ambitious and require outside funding and expertise, or be an activity which can be run through a group's own resources. Below we briefly reproduce ideas about empowerment and group action from Participatory Research in Asia (PRIA) and gender analysis from the Harvard Case Book; the pros and cons of women-specific and mainstream projects from ILO; and guidelines for fund-raising from IFUW (see Annex III for addresses).

The Project Context: Group Action

PRIA is a Delhi-based NGO working with grassroots groups and activists to strengthen their capacities in participatory research, training, evaluation and organization building. It has produced an excellent handbook: *Work and empowerment: management of women's economic activities. A manual for activists,* resulting from extensive practical experience in field visits, workshops, camps and training programmes. It combines practical training guidelines with gender analysis in order to empower women. The chapters cover marketing, production, material management, costing, and organization, and numerous examples, plans, checklists and practical aids all provided. The section on empowerment explains PRIA's approach:

'**Collectivisation:** Bringing a group of women together at a base to become an integral part of an economic activity is an important part of the strategy towards their empowerment.

'**Capacity Building**: Once women start coming together, the next step is to enhance their capacity to work as a group and play different roles, necessary for development and maintenance of the group. It is important that women effectively participate in the process of economic activity. This may entail their capacity-building in the skills required for the economic activity undertaken by the group of women.

'**Ownership and Control:** Once women start acquiring the capacity to work as a group, planning, executing and monitoring the activities, the issue of taking control over the whole activity becomes critical. Taking responsibility of more and more functions in the entire process of economic activity helps them gain control over their ventures.

'**Mediation:** Mediation entails relating with the outside world, with the markets, financial institutions, competitors, suppliers, a host of policy-makers and other important segments of external environment, ie politicians, bureaucrats, officials, etc.'

Gender-aware data collection and analysis

Many agencies are deepening their understanding of women and development by incorporating a gender analysis in their approach (see Chapter 1). For such an analysis to be rooted in reality and of practical use, it is necessary to establish a data base which looks at what women do and why. One method used to organize and present data so that it can be usefully translated into project terms is presented in *Gender roles in development projects*. An approach of this sort is applicable to a range of projects, whether general or women-specific. The analysis has four components:

i) The activity profile, based on the concept of the sexual division of labour, sets out the group's activities by gender, ethnicity, social class, age (or other characteristics) and the time spent on them. Full recognition of productive and reproductive activities is emphasized.

ii) The access and control profile identifies what resources individuals can command to carry out their activities, and the benefits they receive from them. The difference between access to resources and control over them is emphasized.

iii) Analysis of factors influencing activities, access and control, including general economic and political conditions, demographic factors, institutional structures, laws and community norms, education ... The list is quite broad but it thus lends itself to adaptation and development for a range of situations.

iv) Project cycle analysis means that the project should be examined at every stage of its development in the light of the data previously gathered and analysed. [See Catherine Overholt et al, *Gender roles in development projects – a case book* (Kumarian Press, West Hartford, 1984)]

Any one or a combination of parts (i) to (iii) can form the basis of a survey or questionnaire, which, you might use, 1) to establish needs and develop a project; and 2) as part of an educational activity, either as part of the preparatory work, or in the course of a seminar as an awareness raising exercise.

Gathering and sharing information

All women with access to materials and resources can contribute by educating themselves and sharing knowledge with others. It can be useful for women to have

- gender-specific data on the aspects of women's work or other issues which concern you (as above);

- information on other groups activities: what NGOs are working locally? What aspects of their work connect with yours? What are their policies on gender? What are the regional or international links of local bodies, from trade unions to religious associations?

- information on the structures you may be able to use or influence: is there a national women's bureau or council? How does it work and are there any links with the district level? Do any local development officers have special responsibility for promoting women's opportunities? What are the other bodies and structures at all levels which affect the working situation of women?

It is not necessarily difficult or costly to obtain information. Guides such as this book contain sources for material, much available without charge to organizations in developing countries. Most countries have offices, missions, or representatives of UN agencies, donor countries, international NGOs, which have or can obtain useful material, from statistics to training modules. Trade unions may be affiliated to international trade secretariats, which can provide literature and might follow it up with a meeting or seminar.

Becoming 'economically literate': *The Tribune no.42* is devoted to 'Making connections: economics and women's lives', and encourages women to improve their economic literacy – that is, increase our understanding of the economic issues that affect our lives. These may include local planning decisions, changes in the market, government loans, currency devaluations, food subsidies, investment policy, and privatization.

The project: mainstream or women-specific?

Images of the gender role in two ILO projects is a handbook on technical cooperation in the field of employment creation and vocational training, produced to accompany a video of the same title. In it the ILO outlines three different ap-proaches to women's employment-related projects, and shows how all can respond in different ways to women's needs, depending on circumstances: these must be established through a gender-based analysis based on the perceptions and priorities expressed by the women concerned.

1) A women-specific approach: This is appropriate when there is:

- the likelihood that explicit attention may help balance an inequality between the positions of men and women;

- a cultural, religious or social tradition that discourages employment of women side-by-side with men;

- a period of transition in the community that may soon lead to a change in views about women's roles;

- an evolution of women's roles and responsibilities due to demographic changes;

- a need for remedial training for women lacking sufficient formal education.

Advantages include:

- increased responsiveness to women's needs, especially when their capacity to express their own needs is inhibited by cultural factors;

- greater opportunities for women in decision-making and leadership, resulting in increased self-esteem;

- opportunities for women to undertake initiatives conventionally seen as outside their domain;

- increased support for women's institutions.

Disadvantages include:

- a risk of continued isolation of women from general development activities;

- a danger of tokenism resulting from a lack of policy commitment;

- a tendency to incorporate a strong welfare orientation in the project activities.

This approach has been successfully applied in areas such as rural and urban employment, vocational training, co-operative training, appropriate technologies and workers' education programmes.

2) The women's component approach: A separate set of activities for women within a general project – may be appropriate when women need remedial training to compensate for deficiencies in their formal education. Time constraints on women's availability could also make this approach a good choice. The women's component can also be effective if:

- women themselves choose to work separately from men to ensure that their own interests and objectives are reached without interference;

- consciousness-raising and confidence-building among women are encouraged.

Advantages:

- it guarantees access by women to project resources;

- it may give women equal access to the general project's main activities;

- it increases the likelihood that planners will notice the women's work and pay more attention to gender concerns;

- it increases the opportunity for the integration of women's identified needs within the planned activities of the general project.

Disadvantages if:

- poor design or management lead to marginalising women's activities from the project's mainstream activities;

- the women's component is not offered the same resources as the main project, perhaps because it was only included to satisfy a requirement of a national plan or development agency.

3) The general approach: also described as 'mainstream', this aims to give equal opportunities to both women and men. The ILO remains aware that special assurances are often required to guarantee equal opportunities for women in the entire project cycle. The general approach might be appropriate when:

- both men and women have been identified as project participants;

- a precedent for shared participation has already been established;

- information about the planned project activities reaches women and men equally;

- the social norms encourage women and men to work side-by-side.

Advantages when:

- all participants are invited to take full advantage of the project's resources;

- access to and influence on decision-making is increased;

- all participants share responsibility equally.

Disadvantages:

- women may not be able to compete with men for limited project resources because women often lack access to information about their employment or training opportunities;

- women may be inadvertently excluded through location, timing or choice of promotion mechanism if women's participation is not clearly defined at the project design stage.

Raising funds

Lack of financial resources should not be seen as a barrier to all forms of action, for example meetings need cost little or nothing to arrange and run; a small percentage of the profits from an income-generating project may be put aside for group activities; a small levy paid by members; fund-raising activities such as sales. Where a good idea can be put into practice only with the help of finances beyond what a local group can raise, the IFUW has produced guidelines to help organizations seek outside assistance. 'Too often people think that all they have to do is fill in the application form. But the successful fund-raisers are those who go and meet with the staff and find out what they can or cannot do; how to prepare applications to fit the funder's criteria; and what are the issues of the moment.'

There are some basic steps to follow when seeking financial and/or technical assistance:

1) Information-gathering: go through directories, write to institutions, read the relevant literature, talk to contacts.

2) Assessing resources: work out what resources are needed, what are available internally – especially non-financial resources, and what types of outside assistance are required.

3) Select source[s] of funding in the light of what you have learnt about different institutions: these may include the local community, banks, businesses, foundations, religious bodies, NGOs, government departments, UN agencies...

4) Write proposals to relevant agencies: be sure to respond to the funder's criteria, which might include the need for projects to become self-sufficient after a certain time, to reach especially poor or disadvantaged people, to be replicable in other places, to be accountable throughout their term. Include clear information about your group or organization, including membership figures, constitution, legal registration (if relevant), a brief history, brochures and reports produced. Make clear: how the project will be run, monitored and evaluated; how funds will be administered and accounted for; how the project links in

with the local community and responds to certain socio-economic factors or trends, explaining how needs were assessed and objectives determined. [Based on *Successful development of women's international projects: a handbook on the project cycle*, by Theodora Carroll-Foster (IFUW)]

ORGANIZING AN EDUCATIONAL ACTIVITY

Depending on the context and your aims and objectives, an educational activity may be anything from a two-hour meeting to a five-day seminar, an ongoing study circle to an international workshop. The aim of this book is to provide material of use in most situations, whether to devise questions for discussion, or reproduce sections as handouts.

Questions to raise

Many issues are raised in the course of the book: look at the table of contents and index, and decide which are of particular concern in your situation.

In some cases, a trend or issue may have both positive and negative impacts on women, for example: new technology; homeworking, and part-time work. Some themes and issues recur, for example: the role of gender; the sexual division of labour; society's attitudes to work and skills. It can be useful to take these concepts and examine how they shape our lives. Get people to list all their activities over a 24-hour period: this can help them understand their many roles and the range of skills they draw on (and see notes on gender analysis above). They can then divide the activities according to their value and economic reward, and also compare which tasks a man in a comparable situation might perform.

Chapters 2 to 6 generally start with overviews of certain trends, and consider definitions, such as 'informal sector' or 'economic activity'. You could discuss to what extent these apply to your own country, workplace or community. The conclusions then pick up a few of the main points in that chapter, sometimes raising questions – for example, who benefits from industrialization? sometimes making recommendations, for example in relation to rural employment and the informal sector. You can use these as the basis for discussions, asking participants if they agree or disagree with the conclusions and recommendations (if any), and why.

One way of stimulating and focusing discussion can be to develop some type of ranking exercise. An example is reproduced overleaf from the SEAD education pack, *Shoulder-to-shoulder*. You could adapt this for other discussions, such as 'Equal working opportunities for women requires...' and use the points covered in Chapter 2, in particular. Other headings might be 'Human rights for women means...' or 'Education and training for girls and women should include...'.

Different activities

Discussion is only one of a number of possible activities. Role play can be used to explore aspects of certain situations organizing at a workplace, for example, or problems of sexual harassment, or lobbying local politicians. Role play should end with a discussion once participants have shed their 'characters', so that they can unwind and draw lessons from the experience. Drama can also be used as a means of communicating certain educational messages; another possible group activity is the preparation of plays which can be shown at workplaces, union meetings and other gatherings.

Practical tasks can be set, depending on the activity: preparing a resolution or workplace policy statement on sexual harassment, drafting a letter to government ministers on labour laws or standards, making posters setting out health and safety guidelines, writing a leaflet or brochure on equal pay or childcare, listing areas where research or data collection is required, drawing up an equal opportunities programme for trade union or workplace...

Methodology

Whatever the form of the activity, it should give participants the opportunity to explore and understand an issue, making contributions from their own experience. This is known as the active learning or participatory approach. Group work is an important part of this approach, but a well-prepared input is necessary to give groups something to work on. This might be a short presentation by a speaker or panel of speakers, a video or other audio-visual aid, some written material like a newspaper report or case study, even a cartoon or photo. Groups should always note down their main ideas or findings, and come together in a plenary to report back, compare notes, and – where appropriate – develop an action plan, strategy or follow-up.

Modules can be prepared to help structure a programme, whether it is a half-day meeting or full-scale training course. A module could consist of some guidelines for educators to help them present an issue and run a session; activity sheets (see overleaf) for participants with practical guidelines for group work and clearly-defined tasks; a handout with further information, if possible. An increasing number of national and international trade union organizations have developed materials for women's training; you should consult your national union centre, the international trade secretariat for your occupational sector, and/or the ILO.

DEVELOPMENT FOR WOMEN REQUIRES . . .

More and better childcare	Higher living standards	Reduction of domestic chores
Better health care and family planning	A redistribution of the country's wealth	The support of other women
Having a say in the life of the community	Freedom from poverty	Better access to education, skills training and job opportunities

Diamond ranking: Cut up the nine diamonds and arrange in a new large diamond, putting the statement you most agree with at the top and the one you least agree with at the bottom. The others will be arranged in the middle as follows:

MOST AGREE

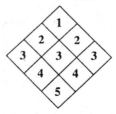

LEAST AGREE

ACTIVITY 15

Understanding Equal Value

Aim

*   To help you understand 'equal value'.

Group Work

1.   Choose two of the jobs you know well (one should be a man's job, one should be a woman's job).

2.   Make a note of all the tasks each worker does.

3.   Make a note of hazards, skills and work involved for each job (remember all the tasks).

4.   Use the chart to decide 'the value' of each job. Are they paid fairly?

Job	Man	Woman
List of Tasks		
Heavy or Light Work		
Many or Few Hazards		
Many or Few Decisions		
Skill High or Low		
Responsibility High or Low		

Equality : The continuing challenge

ANNEX III

LIST OF ORGANIZATIONS

INTERNATIONAL AND INTERGOVERNMENTAL

Commission of the European Communities (CEC), 200 rue de la Loi, 1049 Brussels, Belgium

Food and Agricultural Organization of the United Nations (FAO), via delle Terme di Caracalla, 00100 Rome, Italy

International Fund for Agricultural Development (IFAD), 107 via del Serafico, 00142, Rome, Italy

International Labour Organisation (ILO), 1211 Geneva 22, Switzerland

International Monetary Fund (IMF), 700 19th Street NW, Washington DC 20431, USA

International Organization for Migration (IOM), 17 route des Morillons, 1211 Geneva 19, Switzerland

International Research and Training Institute for the Advancement of Women (INSTRAW), PO Box 21747, Cesar Nicolas Penson 102-A, Santo Domingo, Dominican Republic

Organisation for Economic Cooperation and Development (OECD), 2 rue Andre Pascal, 75775 Paris 16, France

United Nations Children's Fund (UNICEF), 3 United Nations Plaza, New York, NY 10017, USA; and Palais des Nations, 1211 Geneva 10, Switzerland

United Nations Conference on Trade and Development (UNCTAD), Palais des Nations, 1211 Geneva 10, Switzerland

United Nations Department for Social Development and Humanitarian Affairs, PO Box 500, 1400 Vienna, Austria

United Nations Development Fund for Women (UNIFEM), 304 East 45th Street, New York, NY 10017, USA

United Nations Development Programme (UNDP), One United Nations Plaza, New York, NY 10017, USA

United Nations Division for the Advancement of Women (DAW), PO Box 20, One United Nations Plaza, New York, NY 10017, USA

United Nations Educational, Scientific and Cultural Organization (UNESCO), 7 place de Fontenoy, 75700 Paris, France

United Nations Environment Programme (UNEP), PO Box 30552, Nairobi, Kenya

United Nations Industrial Development Organization (UNIDO), Vienna International Centre, PO Box 300, 1400 Vienna, Austria

United Nations Non-Governmental Liaison Service (NGLS), Palais des Nations, 1211 Geneva 10, Switzerland; and 866 United Nations Plaza, New York, NY 10017, USA

United Nations Research Institute for Social Development (UNRISD), Palais des Nations, 1211 Geneva 10, Switzerland

United Nations University, World Institute for Development and Economic Research (WIDER), Annankatu 42C, 00100 Helsinki, Finland

World Bank, 1818 H Street NW, Washington DC 20433, USA

World Health Organization (WHO), 1211 Geneva 27, Switzerland

UNITED NATIONS REGIONAL COMMISSIONS
(all have a women's programme or focal point)

Economic Commission for Africa, PO Box 3001, Addis Ababa, Ethiopia

Economic and Social Commission for Western Asia, PO Box 950629, Amman, Jordan

Economic and Social Commission for Asia and the Pacific, United Nations Building, Rajadamnern Avenue, Bangkok 10200, Thailand

Economic Commission for Latin America and the Caribbean, Edificio Naciones Unidas, Casilla 179-D, Santiago, Chile

Economic Commission for Europe [includes North America], Palais des Nations, 1211 Geneva 10, Switzerland

146

NON-GOVERNMENTAL ORGANIZATIONS

National and international NGOs number many thousands, and only a small selection are listed here. NGLS can put you in touch with organizations in your country and sector of interest.

Accion International, 1385 Cambridge Street, Cambridge, Mass. 02139, USA

African NGOs Environment Network, PO Box 53844, Nairobi, Kenya

American Association of Retired Persons (AARP) and International Federation on Ageing (IFA), 1909 K St NW, Washington DC 20049, USA

American Friends Service Committee (Women's program), 1501 Cherry St, Philadelphia, Pennsylvania 19102, USA

Anti-Slavery International, 180 Brixton Rd, London SW9 6AT, UK

Asia Monitor Resource Centre, 444 Nathan Rd 8-B, Kowloon, Hong Kong

Asia and Pacific Development Centre (APDC), Persiaran Duta, PO Box 12224, Kuala Lumpur, Malaysia

Asian Women Workers' Centre, 2-3-18-34 Nishiwaseda, Shinjuku-ku, Tokyo 169, Japan

Association of African Women for Research and Development (AAWORD), c/o CODESRIA, BP 3304, Dakar, Senegal

Caribbean Association for Feminist Research and Action (CAFRA), PO Bag 442, Tunapuna, Trinidad and Tobago

Christian Aid, PO Box 100, London SE1 7RT, UK

Commission on the Churches' Participation in Development (CCPD), World Council of Churches, 150 route de Ferney, 1211 Geneva 20, Switzerland

Commonwealth Secretariat, Marlborough House, Pall Mall, London SW1Y 5HX, UK

Committee for Asian Women (CAW), 57 Peking Road 4/F, Kowloon, Hong Kong

Development Alternatives with Women for a New Era (DAWN), c/o Asia and Pacific Development Centre, Malaysia (see above)

Debt Crisis Network, 1901 Q St. NW, Washington DC 20009, USA

GABRIELA (General Assembly Binding [Women] for Reforms, Integrity, Equality, Leadership and Action), PO Box 4386, Manila 2800, The Philippines

Grassroots Women's Organizations Working Together in Sisterhood (GROOTS), c/o Jaya Arunachalam, Working Women's Forum, India

GRESEA (research group on trade issues), rue Royale 11, 1000 Brussels, Belgium

HelpAge International, St James' Walk, London EC1R 0BE, UK

Korean Women Workers' Association, Guro-Dong 428-1, 3/F, Guro-ku, Seoul, Korea

KMK (Women Workers' Movement), Room 406, R & G Tirol Building, 831 Edsa Corner, Scout Albano St, Quezon City, The Philippines

Institute for African Alternatives (IFAA), 23 Bevenden St, London N1 6BH, UK

Institute of Development Studies, University of Sussex, Brighton, UK

Institute of Social Studies (Women's Studies Programme), Badhuisweg 251, 2597 JR The Hague, The Netherlands

Institute of Social Studies, 5 Deen Dayal Upadhyaya Marg, New Delhi 2, India

Interfaith Action for Economic Justice, 110 Maryland Ave. NE, Washington DC 20002, USA

International Coalition for Development Action (ICDA), 22 rue des Bollandistes, 1040 Brussels, Belgium

International Council of Jewish Women, 19 rue de Tehran, 75008 Paris, France

International Council of Voluntary Agencies (ICVA), 13 rue Gautier, 1201 Geneva, Switzerland

International Council of Women, 13 rue Caumartin, 75009, Paris, France

International Council on Social Welfare, Koestlergasse 1/29, 1060 Vienna, Austria

International Federation of Business and Professional Women, 8 Battersea Park Rd, London SW8 4BG, UK

International Federation of University Women (IFUW), 37 Quai Wilson, 1201 Geneva, Switzerland

International Women's Tribune Centre, 777 UN Plaza, New York, NY 10017, USA

International Organisation of Consumer Unions (IOCU), Emmastraat 9, 2595 EG Amsterdam, The Netherlands; and PO Box 1045, 10830, Penang, Malaysia

International Restructuring Education Network Europe (IRENE), Stationsstraat 39, 5038 EC Tilburg, The Netherlands

InterPress Service/ Women's Feature Service, via Panisperna 207, 00184 Rome, Italy

ISIS International (Women's International Information and Communication Service), Casilla 2067, Correo Central, Santiago, Chile; and 85a East Maya Street, Thilamlife Homes, Quezon City, The Philippines

Leicester Outwork Campaign, 116 St. Peter's Road, Leicester, UK

MISSIA (The All-Russia Women's Association, ul. Ostrovitjnova 27/1-67, Moscow, Russia

Netherlands Organisation for International Development Cooperation (NOVIB), Amaliastraat 7, 2514 JC The Hague, The Netherlands

Oxfam, 274 Banbury Rd, Oxford, UK

Pakistan Institute of Labour Education and Research, 762-C, Block II PEC, PO Box 8032, Karachi 29, Pakistan

Participatory Research in Asia (PRIA), 42 Tughlakabad Institutional Area, New Delhi 110062, India

Pesticides Action Network (PAN), c/o International Organisation of Consumer Unions, Malaysia (see above)

Rede Mulher, Caixa Postal 1803, 01051 Sao Paulo SP, Brazil

SAGO (International women's solidarity network, Latin America Europe), Lange Lozanastraat 14, 2018 Antwerp, Belgium

Scottish Education and Action for Development (SEAD), 23 Castle St, Edinburgh EH2 3DN, UK

Self-Employed Women's Association (SEWA), Victoria Garden, Bhadra, Ahmedabad 380001, India

Society for International Development (SID), Palazzo Civilta del Lavoro, 00144 Rome, Italy

SOMO (Centre for Research on Multinationals), Paulus Potterstraat 20, 1071 DA Amsterdam, The Netherlands

Soroptomist International, 87 Glisson Rd, Cambridge CB1 2HG, UK

Third World Network, 87 Cantonment Rd, 10250 Penang, Malaysia

Trasnationals Institute, and Transnationals Information Exchange (TIE), Paulus Potterstraat 20, 1071 DA Amsterdam, The Netherlands

Vrouwenbond FNV, Postbus 856, 1005 AL Amsterdam, The Netherlands

WOMANKIND Worldwide, 122 Whitechapel High Street, London E1 7PT, UK

Women's International League for Peace and Freedom (WILPF), 1 rue de Varembe, 1211 Geneva 20, Switzerland

Women Working Worldwide, Box 92, 190 Upper St, London N1 1RQ, UK

Working Women's Forum, 55 Bhimasena Garden St, Mylapore, Madras 4, India

World Association of Girl Guides and Scouts, 12c Lyndhurst Rd, London NW3 5PQ, UK

World Development Movement, 25 Beehive Place, London SW9 7QR, UK

World University Service, 20 Compton Terrace, London N1 2UN, UK

Zonta International, 557 West Randolph St, Chicago, Ill. 60606, USA

INTERNATIONAL, REGIONAL AND NATIONAL WORKERS' ORGANIZATIONS

Caribbean Congress of Labour, 407 Norman Centre, Broad St, Bridgetown, Barbados

Congreso Permanente de Unidad Sindical de los Trabajadores de America Latina (CPUSTAL), Ribera de San Cosme 22/ Office 105, Col. San Rafael CP 06470, Mexico 4DF, Mexico

European Trade Union Confederation (and Institute), 37-41 rue Montagne aux Herbes Potageres, 1000 Brussels, Belgium

International Confederation of Arab Trade Unions, PO Box 3225, Damascus, Syria

International Confederation of Free Trade Unions (ICFTU), 37-41 rue Montagne aux Herbes Potageres, 1000 Brussels, Belgium

International Federation of Building and Woodworkers, PO Box 733, 1215 Geneva 15, Switzerland

International Federation of Commercial, Clerical, Professional and Technical Employees (FIET), 15 ave de Balexert, 1219 Geneva, Switzerland

International Federation of Free Teachers' Unions, N2 Voorburgwal 120 – 126, 1012 SH Amsterdam, The Netherlands

International Federation of Plantation, Agricultural and Allied Workers (IFPAAW), 17 rue Necker, 1201 Geneva, Switzerland

International Textile, Garment and Leather Workers' Federation, 8 rue Joseph Stevens, 1000 Brussels, Belgium

International Union of Food and Allied Workers' Associations (IUF), 8 rampe du Pont-Rouge, 1213 Petit-Lancy, Switzerland

Organisation of African Trade Union Unity (OATUU), PO Box M 386, Aviation Rd, Accra, Ghana

Pacific Trade Union Community, c/o ACTU, 393-7 Swanston Street, Melbourne, Victoria 3000, Australia

Public Services International (PSI), 45 avenue Voltaire, 01210 Ferney-Voltaire, France

World Confederation of Labour (WCL), 33 rue de Treves, 1040 Brussels, Belgium

SELECTIVE BIBLIOGRAPHY

Cornia, G.A., R. Jolly, F. Stewart (eds.), *Adjustment with a Human Face* (UNICEF/Clarendon Press, Oxford, 1987)

Committee for Asian Women, *Many paths, one goal: organising women workers in Asia* (CAW, Hong Kong, 1991)

Chhachhi, Amrita, and Renee Pittin (eds.), *Confronting state, capital and patriarchy: women organising in the process of industrialisation* (Macmillan, London, 1993)

CHANGE – a series of reports on women in different societies, and on issues facing women, PO Box 824, London SE24 9JS, UK

Davies, Miranda, (ed.), *Third world – Second sex* (Zed Books, London, volume 1 – 1983, volume 2 – 1987)

Diallo, Mid, Maurice Dopavogui, Gerard Kester, *Guinée: pour un nouveau syndicalisme en Afrique* (PADEP/ APADEP and L'Harmattan, Paris, 1992)

George, Susan, *The debt boomerang: how third world debt harms us all* (Pluto Press and Transnational Institute, London, 1992)

Griffith-Jones, Stephanie, et al, *Fragile finance: rethinking the international monetary system* (FONDAD, Noordeinde 107A, 2514GE The Hague, Netherlands, 1992)

Hazzard, Virginia, *UNICEF and women: the long voyage*, (UNICEF History Series, Monograph VII, New York, 1987)

Hewitt, Patricia, *About time: the revolution in work and family life* (Institute for Public Policy Research/ Rivers Oram Press, London, 1993)

Huws, Ursula, et al, *What price flexibility?* (Low Pay Unit, London, 1989)

ILO, World Employment Programme research working papers and Women, Work and Development series

International Women's Tribune Centre, *It's our move now: a community action guide to the Forward-looking Strategies* (IWTC, New York, 1987)

Joekes, Susan, *Women in the world economy, an INSTRAW study* (Oxford University Press, Oxford, 1987)

Keyes, Deirdre and Colm Regan, *Forging links, trading places: you and your union's role in global solidarity* (Irish Congress of Trade Unions and Trocaire, Dublin, nd)

King, E., *Educating girls and women: Investing in development* (World Bank, Washington DC, 1990)

Kishwar, Madhu and Ruth Vanita, (eds.), *In search of answers: Indian women's voices from Manushi* (Zed Books, London, 1984)

Korean Women Workers' Association, *When the hen crows: Korean women workers' educational programmes* (CAW, Hong Kong, 1992)

Lewenhak, S., *The revaluation of women's work* (Croom Helm, London, 1988)

Mitter, Swasti, *On organising workers in the informal sector* (ICFTU, Brussels, 1990)

NGO/EC Liaison Committee, *Gender and Development: combating gender blindness* (NGO/EC Liaison Committee, Brussels, 1989)

Netherlands Organisation for International Development Cooperation, *Women on the move: a video about international solidarity on the theme of women's work* (NOVIB, The Hague, 1993)

Panos Institute, *Banking the unbankable: bringing credit to the poor* (Panos, London, 1989)

Pietila, Hilkka and Jeanne Vickers, *Making women matter: the role of the United Nations* (Zed Books, London, 1990)

Raghavan, Chakravarti, *Recolonization: GATT, the Uruguay Round and the Third World* (Third World Network, Penang, Malaysia, 1992)

Rowbotham, Sheila and Swasti Mitter, *Dignity and daily bread: new forms of organising among women in the third world and first* (Routledge, London & New York, 1993)

Sen, Gita and Caren Grown for DAWN, *Development, crises and alternative visions: third world women's perspectives* (Earthscan, London, 1988)

Tinker, Irene (ed.), *Persistent inequalities* (Oxford Univeristy Press, Oxford, 1990)

United Nations, *World survey on the role of women in development* (Centre for Social Development and Humanitarian Affairs, Vienna/New York, 1989)

United Nations Children's Fund, *The girl child: an investment in the future* (UNICEF, New York, 1990)

United Nations Development Programme, *Women in development: project achievement reports* (UNDP, New York, 1989)

United Nations Economic Commission for Latin America and the Caribbean, *Major changes and crisis: the impact on women in Latin America and the Caribbean* (ECLAC, Santiago, 1992)

United Nations Population Fund, *Investing in women: the focus of the '90s*, by Dr Nafis Sadik (UNFPA, New York, nd)

Wallace, Tina with Candida March, *Our work is just beginning: a reader in gender and development* (OXFAM, Oxford, 1990)

Young, Kate (ed.), *Women and economic development: local, regional and national planning strategies* (UNESCO/Berg, Paris/Oxford, 1988)

Young, Kate (ed.), *Of marriage and the market* (Routledge, London, 1984)

Periodicals

Many of the organizations listed above produce newsletters or journals. Some other titles of interest, a number of them with a labour orientation, include

Global Labour, BCM Box 2001, London WC1N 3XX, UK

The Tribune, women and development quarterly bulletin. The theme of issue no. 35 is 'Women, work and trade unions'. Published by the Internal Women's Tribune Centre, 777 United Nations Plaza, New York, NY 10017, USA

International Union Rights, 203 North Gower St, London NW1 2NL, UK

ISIS International, *Women's World and Women in Action* (especially 4/89, Women working worldwide)

New Internationalist, 42 Hythe Bridge Street, Oxford, UK

Multinational Monitor, PO Box 19405, Washington DC 20036, USA

Drops of Sweat, newsletter of women in world market factories and homeworking, c/o K. Rosa, Rabenstrasse 37, 2080 Pinneberg, Germany

SID, *Development* (especially no.1 1990 – Young Women: Production/Reproduction and Life Choices)

Statistics

The ILO produces the *Year Book of Labour Statistics*, as well as a statistical annex to the *World Labour Report*. The UNDP sets out a range of development indicators in its annual *Human Development Report*. The *World's women: trends and statistics* is in the process of being revised and a new *World survey on the role of women in development* is being produced for preparation for the Fourth World Conference for Women.

INDEX